Whiz Bangs & Woolly Bears
Walter Ray Estabrooks & the Great War

Harold A. Skaarup

Writers Club Press
San Jose New York Lincoln Shanghai

Whiz Bangs & Woolly Bears
Walter Ray Estabrooks & the Great War

All Rights Reserved © 2000 by Harold A. Skaarup

No part of this book may be reproduced or transmitted in any form or by any means, graphic, electronic, or mechanical, including photocopying, recording, taping, or by any information storage or retrieval system, without the permission in writing from the publisher.

Published by Writers Club Press
an imprint of iUniverse.com, Inc.

For information address:
iUniverse.com, Inc.
620 North 48th Street
Suite 201
Lincoln, NE 68504-3467
www.iuniverse.com

These stories are based on Walter R. Estabrooks experiences during the Great War. He was there, I was not.
I pass them on to you to choose for yourself what to believe.

ISBN: 0-595-09883-5

Printed in the United States of America

Dedication

For my grandfather, Walter Ray Estabrooks and for all those members of the Armed Forces of Canada whose primary task is to ensure that "this day, nobody dies."

Walter Ray Estabrooks, Royal Canadian Artillery (1906-1919)

Epigraph

Old Hands

"I have seen troops coming out of the line tired and dirty after a big push, make their first halt for a little rest. Sometimes a band would be waiting for them. Marching when not weary and with a good band will give some folks a tremendous thrill. But can you imagine a depleted unit coming out of the line from a hard position, tired, dirty, muddy and lousy, stumbling along just after dark, a few minutes halt just out of maximum gun range? "Fall in. Quick March." Imagine that a band has been waiting for them and what it would feel like as it begins playing "The British Grenadiers." The men would hunch their equipment up higher on their backs and their shoulders would straighten up. They would all have fallen in line four abreast without an order. No need for left-right. The muddy boots would seem to lighten up, and darned if the feet don't seem to get the beat of the music. They are old hands, and would soon be disappearing into the night." Walter R. Estabrooks

What were they?

For the curious, a Whiz-Bang was an artillery shell fired by the Germans. It traveled with great speed, and was fired by a fast action gun. There was not much time to duck as one just heard Whiz. Bang! A Woolly Bear was another type of shell that was used for demolition, and when it burst on impact, it made a big hole and left a tremendous cloud of black smoke. They were slower than a Whiz-Bang and could be ducked by a man with a sixth sense.

Table of Contents

List of Illustrations ix
Foreword xi
Acknowledgments xv
Introduction xvii
Walter Ray Estabrooks 1
Diary Notes and the Official Canadian History of the Great War 7
Order of Battle of the Canadian Army during World War One 95
Background to the Estabrooks family name 101
Epilogue 115
Afterword 117
About the Author 119
Bibliography 123
Notes 125

List of Illustrations

1. Walter Ray Estabrooks, Royal Canadian Artillery (1908-1919)
2. Walter on horseback
3. Portrait of Walter age 94
4. Sarajevo, site of the "shot heard round the world"
5. Working Walter's team of horses, Smoky and Trigger
6. Haying
7. Walter and his cousin Oscar Estabrooks on the Western Front, 1917
8. Wilhelmine Estabrook
9. Hal & Dale Skaarup haying with their grandfather Estabrooks, New Brunswick
10. Artillery Summer Camp, Sussex, about 1912, Walter mounted far right
11. Royal Canadian Artillery detachment, Woodstock, New Brunswick, about 1914
12. Walter Ray Estabrooks with Sam Browne belt, about 1914
13. Sopwith Triplane
14. Fokker Dr.1 Triplane
15. Nieuport 17 Biplane
16. Sopwith Snipe Biplane
17. WWI German A7V tank
18. Frederik C. Skaarup, Denmark & Germany, WWI
19. British & Canadian WWI Mk I tank
20. British & Canadian WWI Whippet tank
21. Walter Estabrooks on leave in France, riding with Amy Johnson and otherCommonwealth soldiers
22. Family visit to Vimy Ridge Memorial, 1960
23. Myrtle Olmstead and Walter Estabrooks, 1919
24. Sean and Jonathan Skaarup, family visit to Vimy Ridge, 1990

25. Major Harold A. Skaarup and Sergeant Chris Free near a disabled Bosnian BVP-1980 armoured personnel carrier (APC), Bosnia-Herzegovina, fall 1997.

Foreword

FOREWORD by: Wilhelmine Estabrook

Every November 11th for 60 years following the Great War my father, Walter Estabrooks, attended the Remembrance Day service in Woodstock, New Brunswick. In later years I accompanied him to these events. He would line up with the other veterans, square his shoulders and march off smartly towards the cenotaph where, a little wobbly, he would stand at attention for the playing of The Last Post and Reveille and for the Laying of the Wreath. A deep and pervading sadness for all those who had lost their lives in battle filled the air.

As the ceremony was being carried out, I gazed at the gray heads and weathered faces beneath the Legion berets and I tried to imagine them as young men going off to war. They had heard and heeded the call to arms. They were familiar with the sounds and the smell of horror on blood soaked battlefields. Their legs, now stiff and aching, were once sturdy and strong as they tramped many miles over foreign soil. The hands, gnarled and folded over canes, walkers and wheel chairs, packed kits, guided horses, loaded rifles, carried the wounded and buried the dead. The eyes, behind glasses, milky with age, had witnessed dehumanising brutality, unimaginable destruction and extraordinary acts of bravery.

These few men with my father, still honouring the war dead after 60 years, were the survivors. Their bones were brittle; their bodies fragile; they were no longer buoyed with the vigour, vitality and muscle of youth. Yet, their indomitable spirit endured.

In 1964, as a gift to my father, I typed and made copies of the diary, which he kept from 1916 to 1919. It had been written on bits of paper and cardboard, in pencil. It was smudged, dampened, faded and stained with blood. (He had left the diary with his sister after the war.

Otherwise it would have been lost when our house burned in 1937. My aunt passed it on to my sister, Beatrice, who likely still has the original.) Copies were circulated among his old comrades, his children and grandchildren.

As I laboured over the diary, with maps and geography books, it began to sink in just how terrible that war was. Aside from the bullets and bombs and mustard gas, aside from the fear and the pain, the dysentery, the miseries of fleas and lice in the muddy, bloody trenches, my father spoke of having friends and comrades killed before his eyes. He talked of the horses they lost, the horses who sometimes saved their lives, and then had to be put down when badly wounded. He talked of the farms and fields destroyed.

Later he told me the following story of his life-long friend Otto's horse:

Shortly before World War I Charlie Gray, a farmer in Waterville, raised some fine French Coach horses. He also raised two sons, Halley and Otto.

At the beginning of the Great War, the army sent men around the area to recruit saddle horses for the cavalry to be shipped to Europe and, among them, they picked up from Charlie Gray, a handsome chestnut mare called Queen.

Otto Gray joined the Canadian Artillery in 1915 and eventually wound up in the 3rd Division in France. At the campaign on the Somme, the 3rd Division lost a lot of horses, including the one Otto was riding. Horses wounded at the Front were generally taken to LeHavre in France where they were patched up and rested before going back up the line. In a prior skirmish in another unit, Queen had been badly hurt. One bullet had gone straight through her mouth, piercing her tongue, and out through the back of her neck. She recovered and was returned to battle.

Otto Gray went out one morning to look at the new assignment of horses and found Queen. He swore that the mare knew him. Otto claimed her and kept her through the duration of the war.

Almost three months after Armistice was declared, Otto received orders that he had a return passage back to New Brunswick. He didn't want to part with his chestnut mare so he checked around to see if he could bring her back. Alas, regulations were such that the horse couldn't be brought back. The cost alone was prohibitive. Besides, the many shiploads of Canadian soldiers came first.

When the war ended all available horses were turned over to the French government to replenish the farms. So early in March 1919 Otto Gray said goodbye to his faithful Queen and returned by ship to Canada.

In his Seventies my father took a trip across Canada, stopping to visit several first war veterans whom he'd kept in touch with over the years. Among them were George Evans, Dick Wickens and Otto Gray.

Nearly every year following the Remembrance service my father would have dinner with Lee Bell with whom he soldiered and neighboured all his life. Lee is often mentioned in his diary.

My father's death on February 14, 1985 at age 94, although expected, was a loss, which I still mourn. All my life he had been the mainstay, the one person to be counted on. With his family gathered round his bed, he slipped quietly through that last long night and just before sun-up, his breathing slowed and slowed and stopped. One second he was there in the room with us, and the next second, we were alone. His soul and spirit had fled.

Except for the years he spent in Europe during World War I my father lived in the same community. He served as County Councillor and as a member of the school board. Those who stopped by to share a little time with Dad during the final six months he was in bed; and all those who offered support during his wake and funeral evidenced the high regard in which he was held.

My father has been gone for fifteen years. World War II vets, even veterans of the Korean Conflict are old men now. And wars still rage around the world.

Any thinking person will find the idea of war abhorrent. As John Fitzgerald Kennedy said: "Unconditional war can no longer lead to unconditional victory. It can no longer serve to settle disputes. It can no longer be of concern to great powers alone. For a nuclear disaster, spread by winds and waters and fear, could well engulf the great and the small, the rich and the poor, the committed and the uncommitted alike. Man must put an end to war or war will put an end to mankind." Alas, it seems there will always be bullies and predators, power-hungry dictators who will not listen to reason. And, unfortunately there are also those who blindly follow wherever these men will lead.

There was much to learn from the Great War veterans and so little time. The opportunity to shake their hands, to appreciate the youth that was taken from them, to thank them for their sacrifices no longer exists. Hal Skaarup's "Whiz Bangs and Woolly Bears," is not only a tribute to Walter Estabrooks, but also an acknowledgement of all those who fought and continue to stand up for our freedom.

Acknowledgments

I would like to thank all those who served with my Grandfather during his experiences in the Great War. I would particularly like to thank my Aunt Wilhelmine Estabrook for her having collated my grandfather Walter Estabrooks' notes and diary, for letting me have a copy of it, and for graciously consenting to write the forward to WB & WB. The diary gave me a window on my grandfather's experiences during the war. It also permitted me to have a good background to the large number of questions I had when I wrote to my grandfather to ask him about his experiences. The diary in fact prompted me to examine all kinds of history from a different perspective. For his letters, stories and encouragement, I would particularly like to thank my now long gone but not forgotten grandfather, Walter Ray Estabrooks. I hope that you find his stories and the extracts from his diary of the Great War as interesting as I did. Harold A. Skaarup.

Introduction

Introduction to WRE and the Great War

Wars and battles are very strange things. Trying to understand how they start, who did what and how one suddenly finds young men and women from North America fighting and dying on the historic grounds of other nations, notably in Europe in the last century, is difficult indeed. Both of my grandfathers, Frederik Skaarup and Walter Estabrooks fought as artillery gunners on the Western front. When you try to unravel how the "Great War" started, it is actually somewhat of a mystery. On Sunday, 28 June 1914 in Sarajevo, Bosnia-Herzegovina, a teenage Serbian named Gavrilo Princip assassinated the Archduke Franz Ferdinand, heir to the Austrian throne. In 1996, while on duty with the NATO-led Peace Stabilization Force (SFOR), I was stationed in Sarajevo for six months and had the opportunity to stand in Princip's footsteps. The entire city had suffered terrible destruction during the war that ran there from 1992-95.

Major Hal Skaarup (fall 1997) standing where Gavrilo Prinzip stood when he fired the "shot hear around the world," in Sarajevo, Bosnia-Herzegovina in 1914.

What had changed from 1914? In the summer of that year, few Canadians would or could have been aware that the spark set off by Prinzip would be one of a number of events that would lead to massive losses of life over the next four years. It unfolded somewhat like this:

The European continent had basically divided itself into two armed camps with Germany, Austria-Hungary and Italy on one side and France and Russia on the other. Both had concerns over power and control and intended to go to war if necessary, to keep as much of it in their hands as possible. Unfortunately for Canadians, who were essentially still a British Colony at the time, Britain was tied to some very serious agreements with other nations, particularly France. Although "Britain had no formal alliance with either side, no one in Canada knew that she did have these informal military understandings with France, and they were to prove almost equally binding."[1]

On 23 July 1914, "Austria, supported by Germany, served a harsh ultimatum on Serbia, and on the 28th declared war. Two days later, Russia, the self-proclaimed protector of the Slav nations, mobilized. On 01 August, Germany declared war on Russia and two days later on France. Italy, claiming that she was committed to support Germany and Austria only in a defensive war, remained neutral until May 1915, then entered the war on the Allied side." [2] Basically, a couple of disparate groups began to play the very ancient and unfortunate game of "you fight me, you fight my gang."

As Europe rushed to arms, Britain mobilized its fleet. Germany invaded Belgium, whose neutrality had been guaranteed by Britain as well as Germany, and on 04 August 1914, Britain declared war on Germany. In 1914, when Britain was at war, Canada was also at war; and there was no distinction, although Canadians believed at the time that Britain's cause (in defence of Belgium) was just. Most however, genuinely believed that the war would be over before they could take part in it.[3]

It never turns out that way. We recently tried to force a group of people to give up their historical holy sites, by bombing them. The soldiers said don't do that, we've been there and it will be very bad business if you don't talk through a solution. The politicians went ahead and ordered the airforce to bomb them anyway, telling everyone it would all be over in three days. After 79 days of bombing a nation about the size of New Brunswick, the most powerful allied forces in the world were only able to knock out 13 armoured vehicles out of a hidden target group of 3,500. We didn't win, and not one of the one million refugees created during the event was helped until long after the damage had been done. No body won.

Taking a number of notes from Canadian historical archives, one can see that "in the First World War the Canadian Corps achieved a reputation unsurpassed in the allied armies." A total of "619,636 men and women served in the Canadian Army in the First World War, and of these 59,544 gave their lives and another 172,950 were wounded." [4]

My grandfather had very clear memories of his experiences in the trenches at Passchendaele and Vimy Ridge during WWI. He also remembered a number of the more interesting events that he took part in overseas. I wrote him a number of letters and have written his experiences down as he related them to me. For this book, I have attempted to weave his recollections into the events recorded in his diary. I have also attempted to provide a brief view on the wider course of the war by also including extracts from the official war records. The data that I gleaned from my grandfather has been collectively placed as a story within a story here, which I call "Whiz Bangs and Woolly Bears."

As a boy I used to listen to his stories while we worked around his two large Belgian workhorses, Smoky and Trigger, on his farm in Carleton County, New Brunswick. The horses generated a lot of "pitchfork and shovel work" for a young fellow visiting the farm, but I learned to like working with the team. We used them to haul the old steel and wood mowing machine to cut hay, then to go around again with a long tined rake to gather it up into neat rows, and a third time to pull a big hay loader to get the hay onto a wagon. A long black fork with opposable tines hung down from the barn roof, and the team driver had to back the horses up to lower the rope and drop the fork into the mound of hay on the wagon. Once the hooks were snapped in place, Gramp would show me how to guide the team to haul the fork full of hay up into the hayloft without tearing it out of the roof.

Running the team

In between these chores, or while we were splitting wood in the woodshed, my grandfather would tell me about his experiences during the Great War.

Haying

Gramp never talked much about the bitter side of that war, although what was left unsaid about the other things that happened at that time led me to ask him more questions. He would often give an interesting answer, based on experiences that had happened to him over 50 years ago, and yet which seemed clearer to him than other events much closer to the present. He could talk about those experiences at great length, although he would sum up the events in his life since then in only a few sentences. Many years later I joined the army, and began to have some interesting experiences myself, and it was then that I began to realize what it was that made Gramp's stories so interesting. It was the telling of the story with a clear and often humorous memory of people he worked with, trained with, and grew to know in a way that only people who have undergone stressful circumstances together can know each other, that made the stories interesting. Remembering those people, their names and their stories was important to him, and so it became important to me as well.

Oscar and Walter Estabrooks, France or England, 1917.

Introduction xxiii

As I grew older, I began to read more about the "Great War" and to develop a tremendous interest in history. I visited European battlefields during Army Staff College training, and tried to get a feel for what had happened to Gramp and other men like him. I also read a copy of his war diary that had been typed up by one of his six children, my Aunt Wilhelmine.[5]

Wilhelmine Estabrooks

I was away at school at the age of 18 when I began to write to my grandfather to ask him for more details about the war and the things that he wrote about in his diary. Although I'm older now, and he's long gone, the stories are still interesting. I would therefore like to share as much of it as possible with you in this diary/narrative/history.

My grandfather, Walter Ray Estabrooks survived and got back to Halifax in 1919 on May 24th, at the age of 28 years. Incredibly, he lived to be 94 years old and still had a clear and vivid memory of the events of the Great War that he had personally experienced. The indelible impression that the left on him was passed on to me while we were working with the horses called Smoky and Trigger. I've not forgotten. I hope my children will read them as you have, and stop to think about the incredible times their great grandfathers experienced, and more importantly, to pass the stories on without having to experience the hardships they endured first hand.

Haying with Gramp (and my brother, Dale, on horseback).

As one of Walter's grandsons, and presently a Major serving in the Canadian Forces, I can only reinforce the importance of learning all that you can from your grandparents while they are alive. Write the stories down, and pass them on to your family along with your own stories. Share them, it's how we learn and grow.

Walter Ray Estabrooks

Walter Ray Estabrooks, son of Joseph Leonard Estabrooks and Catherine Mildred Peed (Kate, first generation Irish) was born 13 November 1890 in Upper Waterville, New Brunswick. His ancestors were Anglo-Dutch Flemings, some of whom had originally immigrated to Boston from Enfield, England in 1660, settling nearby in Boxford, Massachusetts. [6] One of Walter's ancestors was Elijah Estabrooks, who was also one of the first settlers to come to the Saint John River (then in Nova Scotia, now in New Brunswick, Canada) in 1763.[7]

Walter had joined the Artillery in Woodstock, New Brunswick, and served with the 10th Battery in 1912 and 1913 during exercises in Petawawa. He went overseas and served with the 32nd Field Battery, 8th Army Brigade, Canadian Field Artillery, on 24 December 1916. [8]

When I wrote to him about his life before the war, he told me the following:

"When I was a teenager I went to the Upper Waterville School. We did a lot of swimming in the creek. Trout fishing was good then in the brook, and eels were plentiful in the creek. I played baseball quite a lot. We used to play against the Wilmot school and about always got licked. I got to be a good swimmer and skater on ice and rollers. I could strike a ball into the next county but was no good as a catcher. We always played barehanded. Our post office was at Waterville, with mail three days a week. Father always had a spare horse or colt that I could ride three days a week to Waterville and back, a little over four miles after school. I don't think I was ever in a saddle until after I was 15 and went to drill at Sussex with the old 10th Battery 12-pounder muzzle loaders."

When I was discussing the kind of military training we undergo in the Canadian Forces today, I asked Gramp about the military training they had undergone in Petawawa during his pre-war training. He described it this way.

"The training you are going through I would have got a great kick out of 60 years ago. We had our morning run before breakfast. Section gun drill. Riding school. A lot of the farm boys had never been in a saddle, and had to learn to keep their toes turned in and not let the stirrup slide back to the instep straight line from the shoulders, middle thigh and ankles etc. The 18-pounder had to be kept clean and oiled and checked ready for action. Occasional route march and usual fatigues, not too strenuous a life compared to what you are going through. Most of our officer's were as green as we were. I had from two to three weeks a year in the militia from 1906 until the First War."

"I joined the artillery because I had trained in the militia. I trained or drilled as we called it, in the 10th Field Battery from 1906-1914. At Sussex one year, Watson Field, Woodstock, one year at Petawawa in 1912."

Training in the summer in Petawawa "was like a try out for a long distance moving of men, horses, guns and equipment. The country we maneuvered in had been burned over the year before. The dust from the ashes on that sandy soil enveloped us to the extent that our horses sickened. I had my own horse Gillie. He was one of the few that completed the last ride for points that last day."

Artillery summer camp, Sussex, New Brunswick, about 1912.

He also told me about how his artillery battery transferred from New Brunswick to Ontario by the train.

"The battery loaded up on flat and box cars, flats for the guns and box cars horses, six horses in a car. We worked all day in Woodstock loading. Money was scarce. George DeLong and I bought a pound of cheese and 25 cents worth of sweet biscuits and the rest for supper. Left Woodstock about 8 PM on the CPR via McAdam, St John to Sussex, getting there 2 PM the following day. I got train sick, as I had never been on a train before. I threw up cheese and biscuits all the way from McAdam to Sussex. Old Dan Gallagher the cook had brought half a barrel of baked beans from Merburg to Woodstock and on to Sussex. Hot weather the last of June and they were so sour that every one was (sick)."

Artillery personnel, Woodstock, New Brunswick about 1916.

Gramp told me that "that was the only time I was ever really homesick in my life. I got 9th grade with Allan Barter at the home school. That fall I did the chores and ploughed 40 acres with the horses we called Maud and Jess. Went the spring term to Jacksontown for 10th grade. Father moved buildings while I was ploughing to get money enough to pay our board. There were several wonderful girls in the grade. I think it was the best year of my teen-age life. I learned to dance the waltz. There are very few of that class living now."

"I saw my first automobile about 1914. I remember when Queen Victoria died, I think in 1901. The news did not get around to the Atlantic until the next day. I finished 11th grade, which was the end of high school at that time, in June 1908. In the meantime, father had sold our old home and moved here in April 1908, and this has been the only home I have known ever since. I liked it up here, but it seemed a lot longer to walk home from Woodstock Friday nights."

"There were no cars to hitch-hike and I could out walk or run a double tram. 16 miles, 4 hours. Father always gave me a lift back Sunday night. Father always kept workhorses that were good roaders. Winter, to get in Monday morning had to feed horses at four AM, to make it in by seven. I never had over 50 cents a week allowance. I saved up enough to take Jessie Young to the opening of the new Hayden and Glen Theatre. I could only get about the fourth row, the best in the Theatre. Most of the young people had cheaper seats in the balcony. She had an idea the balcony seats were higher, and peeved and peeved about it. I hadn't money enough left to buy treat, so walked her home. That ended that heartfelt romance."

"I don't know how I ever made any impression on the girls. (It helped) if a boy had a decent horse and buggy. I had the best Dad in the world about that. I always found it best not to show off. Be a good skater and dancer, and pretty well keep one's mouth shut made more (of an) impression on the girl that really counted."

Walter kept a diary as a record of his experiences in the Canadian Army during the First World War, which came to be known as "The Great War" of 1914-1918. The opening entry in his diary reads as follows.

The Diary of Walter Ray Estabrooks, 1916—1919

"I, Walter R. Estabrooks, enlisted in the spring of 1916 with the 65th Depot Battery at Woodstock, New Brunswick. Stayed home until barracks (in what is now United Farmers' Store) were completed. Was issued uniform and number 335805, April 9th. Chris Armstrong, Miles Gibson, Dalton Rideout and I were made Sergeants of A, B, C and D Subs. We trained on Island Park[9] until several horses and two guns arrived. Then went under canvas at Carvel's Flat (with) Major Price, Captain Berry, Lieutenants Armstrong, White and Winslow." [10]

Diary Notes and the Official Canadian History of the Great War

To place the events of Walter's diary in context, short summaries of the events that took place at the time are extracted from the official war records and included for general reference. As related in the introduction, in 1914, when Britain was at war, Canada was also at war; there was no distinction, although Canadians believed at the time that Britain's cause (in defence of Belgium) was just. Most however, genuinely believed that the war would be over before they could take part in it.[11]

Canada's militia, of which Walter had been a part, was mobilized through the energy of Colonel Sam Hughes, (mentioned in the diary). Walter had to wait for the medical officer to authorize his release for overseas duty, and so he fortunately missed the initial slaughters of Allied forces and arrived in France when trench warfare had already settled in.

He was 15 when he first went to drill at Camp Sussex, New Brunswick, with the old 10th Battery, using 12-pounder muzzleloaders. In his own words,

"I drew my first uniform in June 1906, a week before going to camp. Dressed up in it as soon as I got home and had supper. Felt pretty big. Harnessed old Maud the bay mare in the single wagon and drove up the road to show off. Met Edna Rockwell at the Primitive Baptist Church. The uniform kind of bolstered my courage, and I asked her to have a drive with me. I could not think of anything to say, so asked her to sing. She sang several old songs. She couldn't think of anything to say either."

Between 1906 and 1914 he trained for two weeks each year at Camp Sussex, New Brunswick, and then went via train to competition shoots at Petawawa, Ontario. While working on the B & A railroad in the spring of 1914 however, he came down with typhoid. Although he was able to go to camp 25 June to July 6th, he could not get by the medical officer until the spring of 1916. He trained in Woodstock, NB (along with six horses and one gun), where he had been a Sergeant in the militia and was an Acting Gunnery Staff Sergeant until he landed in England.

Walter's diary records his experiences from basic training through to the battlefields of France. His early diary entries read as follows.

October 3rd, 1916

Embarked at Halifax on the Missanabi, and with two other troop ships and a destroyer docked at Liverpool.

As I went through the diary entries, I asked a number of questions. Here for example, he explained to me that he had embarked at Halifax on the 3rd of October and crossed to Liverpool on the CPR liner **Missanabi** in convoy with two other troop ships and a destroyer. They went the Northern route near Ireland, and down the Irish Sea to Liverpool. From there they were taken to Shorncliffe camp near Folkestone, where they were billeted in tents. There, on the strait of Dover on clear days they could see across to France.

October 13th

Entrained to Shornecliffe. Billeted in tents. Roll Call in the cobble stone paved barracks' square. Foggy wind blowing in off the North Sea. Stand at attention…answer your names…quick, mark time…stand at ease, etc. until 13th. Shot over miniature rifle range.

While at Shornecliffe, Walter was picked for training on the 4.5" Howitzer. He described these pieces of heavy artillery as:

"A high angle of fire gun with unfixed ammunition. They used one charge for dropping a shell over a nearby hill, two charges for a hill farther away, and three charges for longer ranges, in a flat trajectory.

Compared with the eighteen pound shell, the 4.5 weighed about 24 pounds. The eighteen pound shells were fixed ammunition, as they were in a cartridge case about 20" long and propelled by cordite. The three charges that propelled a 4.5 were filled with cordite, NCT,[12] and TNT.[13]

October 20th

On musketry. With tent crew on Folkestone piquet for having an untidy tent. Classes—Gunnery instruction on 4.5 howitzers. From 6:00 p.m. to 10:00 p.m., visited Caesar's camp, Cheriton.

November 1st

Moved in married quarters—Risboro Barracks.

My grandfather told me that while he had trained in England in October and November, it had rained every night. Sir Sam Hughes had his outfit in tents on Caesar's Plains. He tried to get his men placed in barracks, and had some big brass down to review his outfit. They hovered over his men and congratulated him on having such a robust Canadian regiment that could stand it to be in tents. They could not however, get barracks for them. The men had been standing at attention in front of the individual tents. The big brass ordered stand at ease. Sam called them to attention again. He roared out "From now on, only two parades, church parade and pay parade." He turned quickly and fell on his ass in the mud. In any event, from then on there was only one parade, pay parade.

November 9th
Social evening at Wesleyan Church, Sandgate. Met the singer, Miss Ludlow.

November 13th
Birthday. Parade to dentist. On piquet in the evening…chasing soldiers and girls up from Lower Lees, Folkestone.

November 17th, 1916
Received first letter from Canada.

November 20th
On 24 hour duty guarding one shell-shocked man at Moore barracks hospital. Played checkers with him during the day. Sat with him at meals in a long mess hall. At supper, ate my first rabbit stew. He made up his own cot, found a couple of blankets for me; said he never wakened until morning. I lay down and promptly went to sleep. Waking later…not opening my eyes, I could hear breathing above me. I opened my eyes and grabbed for ankles. Before I had a good grip he sprang clear, and back in bed, dropping my bandoleer he was holding over his head. Needless to say, it spoiled my nap.

November 25th
Marched to Hythe ranges, carrying Lee Enfield rifles and noon rations. Made my best marks on the 600-yard range.

November 25th
Weekend in London. Westminster Abbey. Houses of Parliament, Buckingham Palace. Cleopatra's Needle. Whitehall. Horse Guards. Bank of England Tower of London. London Bridge. Tower Bridge.

November 27th, 1916
Started Howitzer course.

December 8th
Went on leave with Ed Duffy and Lee Bell. Went to London, went to a show. Took late train to Edinburgh. Got rooms at King George and Queen Mary Club. Saw old Scotch Parliament, Statue of Charles First, Tomb of Paul Knox, Edinborough University, National Scottish Museum, Edinborough Castle, and King's Theatre in evening, Art Gallery. Went on bus to fourth bridge. Passed little bridge where Mary, Queen of Scotland met Rizzo and eloped.

December 12th
Came back to London. Visited Royal British Museum, Banquet Hall of Charles 1st. Through Westminster Abby.

December 13th
Went through Tower of London, Regents Park, and Zoological Gardens.

December 17th
Entrained for Southampton. Boarded transport and landed at LeHarve, (France), the morning of December 19th.

He told me about the move as they left Southampton and crossed to LeHarve, France, and went up through Rouen to the front line at Haut-Avesnes. The Canadians had just come off the battles of the **Somme**, and as the 18-pounders needed men, he and his friends Lee Bell and Ed Duffy were attached to the Division headquarters and eventually the **32nd Battery**. There they took part in holding the line on the **Arras** and **Vimy** front during the winter of 1916-1917. They gave covering fire for infantry raids involving the CMR, RCR, and PPCLI.[14] He told me that a typical unlucky night would involve being on a work party to dig temporary emplacements for the trench mortar operating in no man's land, with nothing for protection but a shovel, and nothing to eat from six at night until seven in the morning. In his words, the "mud in the trenches was waist deep, and we spent most of the time dodging Whiz Bangs."

I asked him what a Whiz-Bang was, and drew the response that:

"The Whiz-Bang was a field gun used by the Germans in the forward area as opposed to our 18-pounder. The shells were slightly under 3 feet and longer than ours. They traveled with great speed, and were fired by fast action guns, but did not have the strafing power of our 18's. Not much time to duck as one just heard Whiz. Bang! Our 18-pound shells were filled with bursting charges regulated by time fuse up to 21 seconds, and filled with about 100 steel bound bullets. The Whiz-Bangs were similar except the bullets were lead shrapnel. Our HE[15] shells burst on contact, and were filled with NCT. Woolly Bears were another problem for us".

Needless to say, the use of military abbreviations is not something new, and of course on reading these terms I had to draft another letter, this time to ask about Woolly Bears. He replied that,

"A Woolly Bear was used for demolition, and could be compared with our 5.9's. It burst on impact, made a big hole and left a tremendous cloud of black smoke. They were slower than a Whiz-Bang and could be ducked by a man with a sixth sense".

December 19th
Marched through Haffleur to Canadian Base.

December 20th
Marched down the long steps to rail yards in evening. Entrained, got a little sleep under seat. Arrived Rouen December 21st.

December 21st
Had a good feed at rest camp.

December 22nd

Up the lines. Thirty in a tiny boxcar. Unloaded. Packed. Several kilometres in pouring rain [Haute-Avesnes].[16]

December 23rd

Marched six kilometres (West) to Hermaville in pouring rain. Had to wring out our socks at third DAC (Northwest at) Frévin Capelle. Truck carrying our blankets and kit bags ran over embankment and crashed. Marched to LaHarrset 9th Brigade rear. Cold and wet. Slept on soft side of a brick floor in old sugar refinery.

December 24th

First day with 32nd Battery. Went on guard 6:00 p.m. with Corporal Creighton, Ed Duffy and Lee Bell. A group around singing carols. Some just singing. Machine gun fire up the line. Occasional gun flashes and flares lighting the sky.

December 25th, 1916

On guard. Bread, jam, cold beef, mustard pickles, tea for dinner. Supper—roast beef, mashed potatoes, cake, plum pudding, orange and coffee, (beer if you wanted it).

December 26th

First time on horseback since leaving Canada. Painted wagons with Wheelwright Cook. To dentist and gas school, afternoon.

January 4th, 1917

Lee Bell and I sent to guns with Bdr. Dobson. Joined B-sub. Guns, chalkpits at left of Sainte-Catharines.[17] First night in a dugout. Boys had French bread and Oxo for lunch. Sgt. Cornelia O'Neil, Earnie Bennett, Evan Fitzpatrick, Jimmie Morrison, George Haddock, Dick Wickens, George Evans.

January 9th

Sent in front line with Bdr. Heney and Signaler Whitehouse. Front line full of mud. Got lost but eventually reached telephone station in an old mine shaft infested with rats and lice.

Walter told me that while they were on duty in the dugouts they took turns on watch, two hours on and two off for 48 hours. The dugouts had been an old chalk quarry mine, and were infested with big gray rats. "You had to cover your face when trying to sleep," he said.

January 11th, 1917

On telephone from midnight 'til morning. We were relieved by Corporal Webb and Signaler Boyer.

January 12th

George Smith joined the battery.

January 13th

On carrying party to OP in evening with experienced men. [18] Guide says, "It's dark, be careful. We will go overland from second." We were plodding along in single file… a loud pop up front. Everybody stopped but Estabrooks. He bumped into man leading…each with several sheets of corrugated on their backs. Crash…bang. Everybody flopped as a flare lit the sky. What fool! Did not know enough to stop when he heard a flare pistol. A machine gun sprayed us about a minute. Nobody answered—but I learned my first lesson.

January 15th

Carrying party to OP in the evening. Bosche took a crack at us with machine gun.

January 17th
　Quiet day.

January 18th, 1917
　Battery runner.

When I asked my grandfather about runners and dispatch riders, he indicated that:

"Each of the three battalions that formed the brigade had to supply a man to be attached to Brigade HQ, to be a runner, dispatch rider, go-fetcher. HQ was usually situated out of the line of observation from the front line. We carried orders to Battery Ammunition columns, and met motor cycle dispatch riders at the nearest place they could come. The motor cyclist HQ had three heavy cog drive cycles to be used when necessary. If the trip was not over a couple of miles, I would rather walk than drag a bicycle over rough country to reach a road going the way you needed to go. I could read maps and get to places, so I was unlucky enough to get several of the long distance trips."

About officers, he commented on one particular incident:

"I was accompanying a new officer that I had met in England from the gun position to OP. One of those long-range shells passed over us about a mile in the air. I paid no attention, but he dove for the ditch. By the time the sound got to us it was bursting near our ammo dump about four miles in the rear. He looked funny as he got up from the ditch, but that's when I realized that officers had to grow up the same as men in the ranks."

January 19th
　Fired 18 rounds. Went on guard.

January 20th
Gun laying practice.

January 21st
On party digging trench mortar emplacements. Mail in. Received box from home.

January 22nd
Short strafe. On working party until midnight. Sergeant Davies, Labey, Bert Bryan and two men from left section. When Bert's shovel got heavy he told stories. He was good.

There were lots of storytellers in the lines, and his friend Bert Bryan's stories were some of the best, depending on who the tale was about. This brought us around to stories about Passchendaele, which he described as:

"Passchendaele was just one glorious mud hole. We were there 42 days. Kept 24 men on the guns and lost 42 in the time, an average of one a day". He used the word shocked for one man, which he described as "to be shell shocked, one is just in a daze until it wears off, if it ever does."

January 14th
Sent to Eighth Brigade as runner. Slept in an old pit. Cold.

January 25th
Missed breakfast. Pimm, the HQ cook, gave me best dinner in France. Box from Aunt Edith.

January 26th, 1917
Box from Myrtle.

January 27th
Got paid. Made five trips from HQ to Battery.

January 28th
One trip to Battery. Two to Sainte-Catharines. [19]

January 29th
Plum pudding for supper.

January 30th
Rode bicycle with dispatches to Hermaville.[20] Started to snow. Through Louez, Eturn, Bray, Ecdivres, Aco. Anzin-Saint-Aubin.[21] Returned by Arras-St. Pol Road to Sainte-Catharines. Played out. Left bicycle behind a brick wall, kicked some snow over it, got it next day.

January 31st, 1917
Duffy, Bell and I got our lost kit bags. BHQ left of Arras and Lille Road in front of Sainte-Catharines. [22]

February 1st
Trips to Battery until the 4th.

February 4th
Over to Eighth Infantry BHQ, with Mr. Case. One trip to Anzin to meet dispatch rider. Trips to Battery 'til February 8th.

February 8th
Walked to Mont-Saint-Eloi[23] to Ecurie to dentist.

February 9th
Battery moved to a new position back of Arian dump.

February 11th
 Eighth HQ went out. Ninth took over. Not as good a cook as Pimm.

February 12th
 Built a bivouac, Trips to Battery as usual until February 16th.

February 16th, 1917
 Marched to Amettes to rest.[24] Bennett, Berry and I rode mule train, to Maroeuil.[25] Walked to Camblain l'Abbé.[26] Caught column. Marched all night. First experience with Captain Dick.

February 20th
 Long hard march to Bully Grenay[27] through Ferfay, Camblain Châtelain, Houdain,[28] Barlin, Hersin-Coupigny near Bully-les-Mines, and Sans-en-Gohelle near Liévin.[29]

February 21st
 Mounted orderly to wagon lines.

February 22nd
 Rode little rat-tailed black to guns with orders, to Bully-Grenay, to 8th Brigade HQ.

February 23rd, 1917
 One trip, Forty-fifth[30] rear at Hersin-Coupigny.[31]

February 25th
 On late trip to Hersin. Found 45th officers in Etaminez.

February 27th
 Moved to Amettes.[32] Had dinner in a French restaurant.

March 1st
Still at BHQ. Lots of bicycle riding.

March 5th
Two inches of snow. In to Lillers p.m.[33] Fried eggs and chips.

March 6th
Returned to battery.

March 7th, 1917
Getting ready to move in the morning. George Haddock and I found a place and got double orders—eggs and baked beans.

March 8th
Long march to Guoy-Servins. [34] Guns went in to Ablain-Saint-Nazaire. [35]

As Walter arrived in France, Allied plans were underway for another assault against a German defensive position dug in on Vimy Ridge in North-West France. The Germans had successfully repelled all British and French attempts to secure it to date. The Germans had brought Field-Marshal Paul von Hindenburg and his Chief of Staff, General Erich Ludendorff (the real brains of the combination), from the Eastern Front to replace General Erich von Falkenhayn in this sector. "One of their first acts was to begin the construction of a strong defensive position (known as the Hindenburg Line), behind the River Somme. Rather than fight on the Somme a second time, the Germans then relinquished ground in the spring of 1917 and fell back to the new and shorter line to release 13 divisions for employment elsewhere." [36]

The French, like the Germans, also brought in a new commander-in-chief in 1916. He was General Robert Nivelle, who had been responsible for the successful French counter-offensive at Verdun, and he had a grandiose plan for 1917. He intended to break through the German lines in one bold stroke. In Britain, Prime Minister Lloyd George had replaced Asquith, and, dissatisfied with General Haig's conduct of the Battle of the Somme, made him subordinate to the French general for the attack on Vimy Ridge.[37]

"By withdrawing to the Hindenburg Line in March 1917, the Germans disrupted Nivelle's plan and restricted the French thrust to a sector immediately south of the new Hindenburg defence system. In spite of this, Nivelle directed Haig to open a preliminary offensive in the Arras sector to draw German reserves away from the River Aisne, where the French planned to strike their main blow. Haig planned a double battle to help Nivelle. The Third British Army would mount an attack on an eight-mile long front, astride the River Scarpe, and on the adjoining four miles of front the Canadian Corps would assault Vimy Ridge. [38]

Walter records his participation in this assault as follows.

March 9th
Went up to guns. First good view of Vimy Ridge. [39]

As I scanned through this portion of the diary, I noted that the terrain and battlefields were colourfully described. Souvenirs and living conditions were always of interest. One day he had gone up to a place near Vimy Ridge called "the Pimple" on a foggy morning to take a look at where the French and Germans had fought so desperately the first year of the war. The skeletons were still there, and he noted that there were several V-shaped shields made of oak and steel also still in place.[40] These had been pushed in front of the men while they were crawling forward. The Pimple was under observation and when the fog lifted he didn't stop long. He remembered carrying a beautiful pair of French officer's boots, but after shaking the foot bones out of them, he didn't seem to care for them anymore. He also said that they never could seem to become attached to lice or dirty underclothes enough to regret their passing.

When asked about Vimy Ridge, the subject of "sandbag pudding" came up. It had snowed and rained for a couple of weeks after they had gotten to Vimy. Ammunition had to be packed over roads at night. Their bread rations were put into two sandbag lots slung over a saddle and tied on. The sandbag fuzz worked into the wet bread and it was all one loaf in the bag when they finally got it. Earlier, they had been given a few rations of plum and apple jam. The cook dumped the bread in a big boiler along with a couple of cans of milk and a quart pail of jam, stirred it up and gave them two ladles per ration. His friend Bert Bryan said he ate so much sand bag lint that he never had to wipe himself all the time he was at Vimy.

Rabbit stew brought out another "food" story. Australia shipped an order of frozen rabbits to the commissary as a treat for the soldiers. They were shipped frozen in crates of about two dozen. They had rounded them up in an enclosure, conked them with a club and crated them as they were. By the time they left cold storage until they reached the soldiers, they had thawed out and one could smell the G.S. wagon half a mile away. The cooks and helpers had to wear their gas masks to clean them and soak the carcasses in salt and water for at least 24 hours. He said "they didn't taste too bad if you held your breath."

March 10th

Foggy day. Went on guard. On four hours. Off. Tramped up on the Pimple where French and Germans fought so desperately the first year of the war. Skeletons still there. Some interesting equipment. Several V-shaped shields made of oak and steel, that a man could push in front when crawling along.

March 12

Over to hospital corner in evening with a working party. Horses got bogged in shell holes. Out 'til 5:00 a.m.

March 14th, 1917
On ration party. Carried ammunition to gun position. Usual lot of night firing next three days.

March 18th
To baths in Ablain-Saint-Nazaire.[41] Got a change of clothes at last. The lice were about ready to carry off the old ones.

March 20th
Out in storm with O'Brian to dump at Gouy-Servins.[42] Usual action.

March 24th
Moved to plank road position in front of Mont-Saint-Eloi.[43]

March 25th
Worked at gun pit. Bert Slack wounded at Ablain-Saint-Nazaire. Next three days lot of action. Built a gun pit as near splinter proof as possible. With available material, next few days built bunks in rear of gun pit. Signaler wounded by premature from battery in rear.

April 3rd, 1917
Sky full of planes all day. Lot of firing. Few whiz-bangs were falling short. Carried lot of ammunition.

British and Canadian Sopwith Triplane

German Fokker DR.1

Walter spoke about the aircraft he saw this way:

"Our planes at that time were nearly all two wing. Through all of 1917 the English came over with Triplanes. They were slow, but at full speed would take altitude quickly giving the allies an advantage in the dogfights. The German ace Baron Von Richthofen's squadron was painted a bright red. Our planes had red, white and blue circles (like a target). The German (aircraft had a black cross). We could always tell the German planes by the sound of the motors. Before the Triplane the dogfights were all on our side of the line. After (Gunfire?) brought down Baron Von Richthofen the fighting was mostly on the other side. There were many mistakes made by aircraft, especially after nightfall."

British, French and Canadian Nieuport 17

British and Canadian Sopwith Snipe

April 5th
On working party to OP. Saw infantry over on a raid behind our barrage.

April 6th
Two planes came down in flames up front.

Gramp told me about some of the weapons he trained with, and spoke about his attempts to fire back at German aircraft that attacked them:
"All rifle training in the army was with the 303 Ross and 303 Lee Enfield. Also had a course in the Lewis 303 machine-gun. I blazed away at lone flying German planes when they flew low. I had my gun pinned in the top of a post and when Fritz flew over us, every body ducked but Estabrooks. They often strafed our 18-pounder. The 18-pounder was 3.03 bore compared with the .303 rifle. I had training on old muzzle loader cannons at Sussex back in 1905, and from 1906 to 1914 had two

weeks training at Sussex camp, and competition shooting at Petawawa, taking about a week away from home. All 18 pounders were equipped with a #7 dial sight."

April 7th
Lot of firing. Fritz put over shell gas in the evening.

April 8th
Shelled quite a bit. Len Smith wounded—gun pit across (yrack?) hit twice. Stretcher-bearers busy. Getting ready for big strafe.

April 9th
Big strafe started 5:00 a.m. Took turn at gun laying. Prisoners started coming along, herded by one of our walking wounded. Back to Mont-Saint-Eloi. Met Bill Dawson. Went on guard that night.

April 10th, 1917
Back to dressing station to meet brigade runner. Battery started moving ahead.

April 11th
Moved ahead to Bethune Road left of Neuville-Saint-Vaast. Dug in lot of ammunition left in gun pits. We got hold of two small flat cars. Used them 'til dark. By this time, about six inches of snow had fallen. I was left to guard the cars. A couple of left section boys to guard the ammunition. We upset the cars in shell holes. Piled snow over them. Moved the ammunition into the least damaged gun pit and took our shift four on and four sleep, until we were relieved by working party next morning.

April 12th
B. Sub gun went to ordnance. Lieutenant Clark sent me to wagons lines at Guoy-Servins about eight miles each way through snow, slush and mud. I did not need rocking that night.

April 13th
Enemy out of range. Moved ammunition all day. YMCA set up field canteen at Neuville-Saint-Vaast. Had feed—peaches and biscuits.

April 14th, 1917
Rested part of the day. Packed up to cross No Man's land and left position. To cross No Man's land and the ridge before morning, we advanced by way of Ecurie.[44]

April 15th
Crossed the battlefield of Vimy Ridge. The road had been so badly torn up by our shelling, the holes filled with mud and slush, that we had to relay the guns ahead for short distances with six teams. The dead had not yet been buried. Reached Vimy 12:00 noon. Took up position southern end of town. Lived in an old house while digging in. Wattie Waddell wounded.

Walter described Vimy Ridge to me as,
"Having an easy slope from the Lorches valley on our side, fairly steep on the eastern side, looked like an ordinary piece of farming country at first look. The German front lines and ours were on a slight valley on the western side. Our guns ploughed the whole western side and top over to the village of Vimy on the eastern side".

April 16th
Again in action. Sgt. O'Neal and I had a close call from a 5.9. Robert Deware killed repairing wire front of Vimy. George Haddock and I carried him back to gun position. Burial service conducted by Captain Dick. Later moved to cemetery. Harry Bryan shocked in front of B. Sub gun. Morrison and Wickens got boxes of candy.

April 17th, 1917
  To 22nd. Shelling and being shelled. Gas over every night. Fritz plane strafed us. Blazed away at him with rifle. Got struck on head with a chunk of mud. Morrison got a nasty scratch.

April 23rd
  Up 4:00 AM. Put over 116 rounds. Gas thick all afternoon.

April 24th
  Up to WIT. At railroad. On telephone most of the night.

April 25th
  Plane came down in flames. Went back to canteen west of Neuville-Saint-Vaast. Bought a sand bag of chocolate biscuits canned fruit. The first week in Vimy, rations were packed over the ridge at night on horse or mule back. The bread was put in two sandbags and thrown across a saddle. It rained every night and the drivers came down over the hill on the run. The bread got wet and was a sodden mass on arrival—the jute fibre from the bags well mixed in. The cook dumped it in a big boiler, added a little water and a half pail of jam. We were soon fed up on sandbag pudding and the little extra from the canteen was appreciated almost as much as a box from home.

April 26th, 1917
  Next four days ... give and take. We were gassed about every night and had to retaliate while wearing gas masks. First division infantry had a rugged time up front. Heavy casualties reported. Reid gassed night of the 29th. Feed from canteen night of 30th.

May 1st
  Had to stand to, stand by for nearly five hours with masks. Lieut. Pete Cornel ordered a roll call parade seven o'clock. I was late getting on

parade. Pete stopped in front of me. "Estabrooks, did you shave this morning?" "No sir." "Did you wash this morning?" "No sir." "Sergeant Major, see if you can't find something for these two boys to do." He had caught another in the left section. ("Just what I need, sir! To clean up the ammunition that did not explode in that pit that was blown up!")

May 2nd

Haddock and I took Jimmie Morrison to railhead dressing station, sick. He never got back to 32nd. He was a good soldier, and could sing Lauder's songs a little better than Harry.

May 3rd

Lots of night firing. Gas about every evening. Fixed better emplacements for the guns. Carried steel rails and oak ties to make our dugout splinter proof. Signalers shelled out of their dugout under an old house, night of the 10th. C Sub. Shelled out of their dugout, night of the 11th. Two signalers wounded night of 13th. Went back to wagon lines.

May 14th, 1917

Out herding horses back of Berthonval Wood. E Sub gun hit several wounded.

May 15th

F Sub gun put out of action. Duties around lines. A lot of Carleton County boys looked me up. To dentist, 19th.

May 20th

Sent back to guns. Chris Armstrong and I tramped boldly over the ridge in daylight. Fritz tried us with a whiz-bang. I was nearer the shell hole. Chris claimed he made 14 feet from the time we felt the shell coming 'till we were into the shell hole, and the whizbang burst a few yards beyond us.

May 21st

D Sub dugout blown up—interrupting a 'Penny Ante' poker game. Dugan stayed long enough to show a pair of deuces and picked up the 2, 5, 10 centime and half franc piece on the blanket.

May 22nd

Feeling rotten but kept going the next week. Went down the line. Must have had a touch of trench fever.

May 31st, 1917

I looked up the Tapley boys. Rideout, McLeod, Lutes, McFarlane, Cronkite, Bingham, Kidney brothers, Staires and Monteith from old 65th.

June 1st

Went up the line. Tony Gibbs killed that night.

June 2nd

Got ready for strafe. Stood to until 2:00 a.m. Went back to wagon lines. Herded mules. Went to dentist. Helped get ready for tournament on the 9th. 32nd made good showing.

June 9th

George Haddock wounded in B Sub gun pit.

June 14th

Worked on show wagon. Went up the line at night.

June 15th

Strafe in the night. Played checkers with S. M. Donaldson. Next week we strafed the Bosche and he strafed us.

June 22nd
Greg sent to hospital sick.

June 24th, 1917
Whiz-bang bounced off E Sub dugout. 33rd and 45th shelled.[45]

June 25th
Inspection by General Mitchell. B gun out of action. SOS

June 27th
Limber gunner. Took gun (10 km West) to Ordinance at Villers-au-Bois. About a dozen guns in line up ahead of me. Kept gun coming ahead in line, and worked in shops with Joe McMaster until I returned with it to battery. Now out on rest at Berthonval farm.

I asked him about the task of working as a limber gunner, and he proceeded to describe his duties in this capacity as follows:
"The limber gunner services the gun. He takes charge of loading kits and equipment, so the limber is excused other fatigues. When his battery was loaded at the train station, they were loaded up on flat and box cars, flats for the guns and box cars for the horses, six horses in a car".

July 9th
After two bad days in position embankment, left front of Vimy station.

Some time during this period, Walter observed King George and several members from the Labour Party walked over the ridge from La Targett in steel hats and civilian clothes.
"I was on orderly duty, passed through them going down and when they were coming back everyone one of them had some kind of a souvenir, an old rifle barrel, empty shell case etc. I also heard Sir Robert Borden at Lincquiser on Canadian Sports Day. It would take too long to tell it here."

Vimy Ridge

The official war records indicate that the Canadian task to assault Vimy Ridge "was formidable. Vimy Ridge reared out of the plain like a whale, humped in the north, then tapering off gradually until it finally disappeared in the Scarpe valley in front of Arras. The highest points, Hills 145 and 135, dominated the surrounding country, and the irregular slopes of the ridge favoured the enemy. The western slope, up which the Canadians would attack, though gentle, was very open and could easily be swept by fire. The reverse slope, on the contrary, was almost precipitous and well wooded, providing excellent shelter for reserves and guns." [46]

"During the previous two years these natural advantages had been greatly enhanced by the Germans who had fortified the ridge with successive lines of well-wired trenches, deep dugouts with interconnecting tunnels, and concrete strongpoints. Vimy was a keystone in the enemy's western wall, for hot only did it protect a vital mining and industrial district of France, then in full production for Germany, but it also covered the junction of the Hindenburg Line with the defences running south from the English Channel. It would be impossible for the British to hold ground in the Arras sector in Vimy Ridge remained in German hands." [47] The Canadians would have a difficult task to achieve in capturing it.

"Sir Julian Byng's planning was very thorough. All four Canadian divisions would attack simultaneously in line, with the 4th, the 3rd, 2nd and 1st from north to south. In each case the final objective was the far side of the ridge. Each division came into line on the front assigned to it so that the men could have a good look at the ground. Then they were withdrawn again to rehearse the attack over a full-scale model on which German trenches and strongpoints, kept up to date from ground reconnaissance and air observers' reports, were clearly marked. Training was intensive and realistic, and constant repetition made every man familiar with the ground and with the tactics that would be expected of him in the real attack."[48]

At night "tunneling companies dug miles of subways through which troops could move to and from the front line in safety. Chambers for brigade and battalion headquarters, dressing stations for the wounded and great caves for stores were carved in the walls of the tunnels; all had piped water and electric light. Roads and light railways were built in the Canadian forward areas to bring up ammunition, engineer stores and rations. The signalers were no less busy. To existing telephone circuits they added 21 miles of cable buried seven feet deep to protect it from shelling and installed more than 60 miles of unburied cable along the tunnels and trenches." [49]

Enough artillery was provided to Byng to give twice the density of fire that had been available "at the Somme. A new fuse, designed to burst above the ground, would cut the German wire for the attacking infantry. Great emphasis was placed on "counter-battery" fire to locate and destroy the enemy's guns just before the attack. Finally, and most importantly, a deception plan was designed to ensure that there would be no noticeable change in artillery activity, even on the day of the assault. The preliminary bombardment would last several days, and be maintained right up to zero hour." [50]

"Easter Monday 09 April 1917, was chosen as the day of the attack. The preparatory bombardment began on 20 March, but to conceal the full extent of the massive artillery support available, only half the guns were used during the first two weeks." On 02 April a weeklong pounding of the German positions began. "On the night of 08 April, the infantry moved forward through gaps in the wire to occupy jumping-off positions in No Man's Land. The moon was just past full and partly clouded over," screening the tense lines of waiting men. In front of them shells burst along the dark ridgeline as towards morning the weather turned bitterly cold. Frost covered the torn-up ground.[51]

"Zero hour was at half-past five. At about four, a raw wind blew up, darkening the sky with clouds and covering the Canadians' backs with snow. The attack began exactly on time in the dim half-light, while slanting sleet blew in the faces of the Germans. 15,000 Canadians surged forward in the first wave, closely following the line of the artillery barrage which rolled towards the ridge in precisely lifted increments of 100 yards." Two other follow-on waves of infantry followed. [52]

"The first wave found the defences smashed and the wire effectively cut. Only a few sentries were above ground in the battered front-line trenches; they were quickly dispatched, and guards were posted at dugout entrances until the mop up wave arrived. The lead troops swept on to the second line where, although many Germans were trapped below ground, there was some hand-to-hand fighting before the attackers again moved forward."[53]

German distress rockets were launched into the grim morning sky, but the Canadian counter-battery fire had already disabled much of their artillery. Much of the fire from the few guns the Germans were able to bring to bear fell behind the attacking troops. Gradually however, the hostile fire began to increase, thinning the ranks of supporting units. "Beyond the second line, the infantry encountered determined opposition from well concealed snipers and concrete machine-gun posts, and losses began to mount. On the lower slopes and across what had been No Man's Land, columns of prisoners were collected and marched to the Canadian rear area under escort, while stretcher-bearers carried the wounded, messengers moved through the lines, and supporting troops brought up mortars, machine-guns, picks, shovels, ammunition, water and grenades for the task of consolidation." [54]

"The Canadians reached the crest shortly before eight o'clock in the morning, but hard fighting still lay ahead. On the steep reverse slope the enemy opened up with machine-guns and field guns at pointblank range. In spite of this, the troops plunged downhill in a raging blizzard, overran the batteries, and seized the sheltering woods. By early afternoon most of the Corps final objectives had been taken."[55]

The highest point on the ridge, Hill 145, still held out until the afternoon of the 10th. After two separate attacks, the summit was finally cleared and the ground captured on the far side. This placed the four-mile length of Vimy Ridge entirely in Canadian hands. Artillery still had to be brought forward however, to smash any counter-attacks that might develop and to capture two adjacent features known as "the Pimple" and the Lorette Spur.[56]

"The Battle of Vimy Ridge had been a striking success, and by far the greatest British victory of the war up to that time. The Canadian Corps had overcome one of the most formidable German defensive positions on the Western Front, and Ludendorff, who celebrated his 52nd birthday on this famous 9th of April, confessed that he was "deeply depressed." The Canadians captured some 4,000 prisoners, as well as 54 guns, 104 trench mortars and 124 machine-guns, at a cost of 3,598 fatal casualties. The Canadian memorial presently standing on Vimy Ridge was ceded to Canada by France in perpetuity. It is sited on top of Hill 145, the highest point of Vimy Ridge."[57]

Late in April, the Canadians fought through the area of Arras, capturing Arleux and Fresnoy in some of the hardest and most unrewarding fighting of the war. The French Government replaced Nivelle with General Henri-Philippe Pétain on 15 May 1917, and this freed General Haig to launch an offensive of his own in Flanders.[58]

Following their experience at Vimy, Walter's gun detachment was sent on a short but well deserved rest. His diary entries for the period read as follows.

July 16th
Still on rest.

July 20th

Sports day. Ball game, 22nd and 24th. (9 to 7). Painted guns and wagons a design to camouflage and confuse photography from the air. Rabbit stew supper, 25th.

July 31st, 1917

Big push from Lens to the coast. Six weeks of rain and mud. Usual wagon line fatigues. Getting ready for inspection, etc. Stayed out of line all of August to August 25th.

August 25th

Went into position, front of Maroc among the slagheaps and right rear **Hill 70**. Wagon lines at Boueffles. Gun crew: Corporal Rothwell, Bdr. Grant, Evans, Fitzpatrick, Davies and limber gunner Estabrooks. Position shelled off and on day and night. Carried ammunition. Retaliated with little aviation.

Hill 70

The official war record states that on 07 June 1917, "the Second British Army captured Messines Ridge near Ypres, and while Haig was preparing for the main Flanders offensive, he ordered General Sir Henry Horne's First Army (which included the Canadian Corps), to hold the Germans on its front and prevent them from reinforcing Flanders. On 06 June, when Byng was promoted to command the Third Army, Currie replaced him at the Canadian Corps. This was the first time that the Corps had a Canadian commander. Early in July, Horne handed Currie his first major assignment as Corps Commander. Currie was to break through the Méricourt trench south of Lens and then go on to capture the city. On 10 July the Canadians began to relieve the 1st British Corps opposite Lens and Hill 70."[59]

"After looking at the ground, Currie pointed out that the Canadians would be pushing forward into a low and exposed area dominated by two German-held heights, Hill 70 to the north and Sallumines Hill to the south-east. Unless at least one of these two features would have to be captured before an attack on Lens would be practicable. Currie recommended the capture of Hill 70, and although Haig was convinced that the Germans would never let them have it, finally sanctioned the attempt."[60]

Hill 70 was "a bald dome of chalky downland," and although it "was not very high, it directly overlooked the ruins of Lens and provided observation over the Douai Plain beyond. Its possession by the Canadians would be intolerable to the enemy. Aware of this, Currie decided to use it to his advantage, confident that the Canadians could take the hill. He would then set up an artillery killing-ground for the German infantry moving forward to counter-attack. Artillery bombardment preceded the assault and 3,500 gas drums were fired against the hill and into the enemy reserve positions in the town and its suburbs. At dawn the bombardment included 500 drums of blazing oil projected at selected targets to build up a smoke screen and to demoralize the defenders."[61]

"The infantry assaults went in at first light on 15 August. There were two of them, with the main thrust against the hill by the 1st and 2nd Divisions and a diversionary blow directly on Lens by the 4th Division. The ten assaulting battalions hugged a rolling barrage provided by more than 200 field guns and within 20 minutes had gained the crest. By six o'clock most of the hill was in Canadian hands. The 2nd Brigade however, was held up in front of a well-defended chalk quarry where machine-gun fire cut the Canadians down in swaths. This forced the soldiers to rush from shell-hole to shell-hole, and only after repeated attacks was the 2nd Brigade finally able to clear its front on the night of the 16th."[62]

The enemy struck back with great strength and determination as had been expected. By the night of the 18th, when they at last admitted defeat, the Germans had put in 21 counter-attacks against Canadian strongpoints which were well dug in on the newly captured hill and reinforced with Vickers machine-guns in close support. From the top of the hill, artillery observers could clearly see the enemy's movements, and any concentration of troops brought down a cascade of shells, breaking up attack after attack. The gunners never had better targets. In spite of well-directed artillery concentrations and machine-gun fire however, some of the Germans got through. Resolute German soldiers wearing and carrying heavy flame-throwers, swept the Canadian parapets with sheets of fire. Stick-grenades lobbed into the trenches were closely followed by assaulting forces. Although whole sections of trench were entered and hand-to-hand fighting continued almost non-stop for four days and three nights until the 18th, Hill 70 remained in Canadian hands.[63]

"The fighting around Lens continued until 25 August, as the Canadians cleared the suburbs of the town, but since artillery had been transferred to Flanders, it was not feasible to capture Lens with the few guns remaining. After the 25th, the battle lapsed into a stalemate. During the period from 15 to 25 August the Canadian Corps had incurred 9,198 casualties against an estimated 20,000 for the Germans. Six weeks later the Corps moved to a grimmer battlefield in Flanders."[64]

During the period of the battle for Hill 70, Walter made the following record.

August 31st
Went on battery. Orderly for 24 hours

September 1st
Returning to battery along parapet side of an old German trench. A woolly bear burst directly overhead. Made my first duck without a mind order. Muscular action absolutely. To the bottom of the trench.

September 2nd
Enemy hostile all day. Blew side out of A Sub gun pit. Cleared out from 9:00 a.m. 'till 4:00 p.m.

September 4th, 1917
In to Bully Grenay carrying party. Some of the boys absorbed a few French beers. Strafed by the Bosche from midnight until 3:00 a.m., with shrap, gas and high explosive. Most concentrated fire ever in. George Smith and Bob Harris were back on carrying party without masks, and got quite a bit. Wore our masks on the guns, three hours. Night of the 5th, slept with our masks adjusted.

September 6th
Enemy got hostile, 10:00 am. Kept it up all day. Put two in the cookhouse. The cook had cleared out, and blew up 1000 rounds of ammunition for us. The cook shack did not amount to much, but we missed it.

September 7th
On battery runner. Three trips to brigade.

September 8th
Down to swimming pool at Maroc, and to Bully Grenay with Herb Grant. 9th, 10th, 11th and 12th—quiet. Guess Fritz thinks we are all dead.

September 13th
Moved guns to wagon lines in the night. At Boueffles all day.

September 15th, 1917
Went with Mr. Cornell, Bennett, Dougherty, Frank Smith, and Wickens to get ammunition wagon out of trench. Pulled it to Maroc.

Hooked it behind a lorry, and gave it a merry ride to Bully Grenay. Had feed of eggs.

September 16th
 Moved wagon lines to Pendu dump.

September 19th
 Down to Amettes to hand over guns. Long ride on lorries.

September 20th
 Bob Harris, Frenchy Herault, Ed Duffy and I entrained at Aubigny for ten days leave. Arrived at Paris 8:30 PM. Gare du Nord. Taxi to Hotel de L'Empire. From there to Hotel Brittanique. Had dinner with Price, MacMillan, Booth, Gourlay, Ashton, and Fraser.

September 21st
 Rode metropole to Gare de Lyon. Entrained for Southern France. Passed through Lyon. Stopped in Marseille a few hours. Had a feed at a restaurant near station. In Nice, 3:30 morning of September 23rd

September 23rd, 1917
 Sgt. Major O'Connor, Staff Sergeant Cooper from Ordinance, Ed Duffy and I got rooms at Thiers Hotel. Swam about every afternoon. Theatre in the evenings.

September 25th
 Hired car. Made trip to Italian border, through casino, Monte Carlo.

September 27th
 Entrained by Miss Findlayson from Victoria, BC. A trip through the mountains. Came down to Monte Carlo and had afternoon tea at Café de Paris. Visited casino again, but were not allowed to play.

Gramp spoke of Miss Findlayson in his letters:

"Mrs. Findlayson was a rich woman, touring in Algiers when the war broke out. Her nephew, Captain Findlayson came to France with the first contingent. She sold her business and crossed to Nice to be in the same country with him. He was badly wounded soon after getting to France. She had him transferred to hospital there and stayed with him until he passed away. I located some boys from the platoon he commanded, and told them to give her a good spiel about the Captain. She took four of us for a day through the Alps. We visited the casino at Monte Carlo, had afternoon tea at the Cafe de Paris. (She) paid the tab and gave each of us half a dozen packages of Sweet Cap cigarettes."

September 29th
Down to California beach. Afternoon tea at Vogarde with Miss Findlayson. Excelsior Theatre in evening.

September 30th
Started back up the line. Arrived Paris, morning of October 1st.

October 2nd
Back to wagon lines. Usual duties. Exercise rides, 'till Oct. 9th.

October 9th, 1917
Moved to Fort George.

October 10th
Went to Amettes for guns. Next few days painted guns etc.

October 16th
Took gun to Ordinance, Villers-au-Bois. Had feed of eggs. Went into position, left of Petit Vimy in night of 17th.

October 19th
Bennet in charge. Haddock, Evans and Estabrooks for crew. Fired one round.

October 24th
Pulled guns out of action.

October 25th
Marched to Estra Couchy.

October 26th
Took motor lorries for Belgium. Bethune, Merville, Steenvoorde, to wagon lines at Watou.[65] Fixed horse lines next three days.

October 29th, 1917
Horses arrive. In town with Bennet and Brown.

Passchendaele
The official war record describes the Third Battle of Ypres, better known as Passchendaele, began on 31 July 1917 with a British assault on the German positions. A preparatory bombardment of four million shells churned the reclaimed bogland into a self-inflicted obstacle that drowned men and tanks until the offensive petered out on 02 August. A second British attack under General Gough on 16 August also failed with terrible losses. The offensive stalled, and to add to the misery, the rains began in October. In spite of these setbacks, Haig was determined to capture Passchendaele Ridge before winter set in. On 05 December, Haig decided to employ the whole Canadian Corps in the Salient. After Currie had objected to serving with General Gough's Fifth Army, Haig placed the Canadian Corps in General Plumer's Second Army.[66]

The Canadians therefore returned to Ypres in the middle of October 1917, marching through drizzling rain into a desolated battlefield of water and mud. On 18 October they reached the line they were to take over from the Australians, in a position just forward of the same line that Canada had taken over from the French just before the gas attack at the Second Battle of Ypres.[67]

"The whole area was covered with water or mud so deep that men had to move at a snail's pace, often being forced to wade up to their waists (and that was on the firmer ground). In some places, even the infantry could not cross the half-mile-wide bogs. Guns had to be bunched together in highly vulnerable clusters because it was almost impossible to move them. Without firm ground platforms to fire from, a single round would cause the guns to move or sink. This caused their rates of fire to be very slow, and the guns also had to be constantly re-aimed. The Germans sat on higher ground overlooking this terrible morass."[68]

"General Currie protested to Haig that no men should be called upon to attack under such conditions, saying that the operation was impossible, except at great cost, and futile. He put the cost of the attempt at 16,000 men and asked if success would justify the sacrifice. Without giving reasons, Haig overruled him, but Currie determined that the preparations would be very thorough to give the men a fighting chance."[69]

"More than 100 field guns "taken over" from the Australians could not be found in the waste of swampland, but at Currie's insistence the deficiency was made good. Firm gun platforms were constructed at various forward sites and connected by roads. The well-tried method of placing a curtain of fire between the enemy and the advancing infantry would be followed, but since to predict the rate of advance over that terrain was quite impossible, artillery observers would move with the attacking troops to modify the barrage where necessary and keep it just ahead of the infantry. The front was still a mile from Passchendaele village, and behind the front stretched six miles of shell-ploughed swamp to Ypres. Currie ordered roads, tramways and light railways constructed for bringing up reinforcements, munitions and supplies and for evacuating the wounded. Prior to this, to bring back a wounded man had taken 14 hours of plodding and slipping in the mud. Canadian and British engineers worked day and night to complete the task, suffering more than 3,000 casualties" in the process.[70]

"Despite the meticulous preparations, the operation was incredibly difficult. Ground conditions were at their very worst. The front had narrowed to a salient, vulnerable from three sides. Only two plank roads, accurately marked and shelled by the enemy, crossed the swamp to the front line. Ahead, the German checkerboard system of pillboxes showed only a few feet above the ground."[71]

There was one other change from previous methods of attack. In the past, the troops had been brought up from rest areas just before zero hour, but under the terrible conditions of ground at Passchendaele this meant that the soldiers often arrived more tired than the troops that they were relieving. The Canadians came in four days early to recover from the arduous march forward and to study the ground over which they were to attack. The attack was set for 5:40 AM on 26 October.[72]

"The first phase consisted of a limited assault by the 3rd and 4th Divisions to carry the front forward 1,200 yards. The troops shivered through the night in brimming wet shell-holes. At zero hour they moved slowly forward in a cold, wet mist, having first shed their greatcoats to save as much weight as possible. The barrage, much thinner in these conditions than at Vimy and Hill 70, came down perfectly. Platoons floundered towards the pillboxes, which claimed a heavy toll. Some of the Canadians returned the German fire with Lewis-guns and rifle-grenades, while others worked around to the blind side of the pillboxes to toss grenades through the firing slits."[73]

"The mist turned to rain. There could be no concerted rush forward over the sodden ground, but the line inched almost imperceptibly forward as the men fought their way through the mud to higher ground. Some gained the crest, only to be driven back by German counter-attacks. After three days, the limited objectives remained untaken and the men could do no more. They had suffered almost 2,500 casualties only to win a strip of slightly higher and drier ground."[74]

"Currie ordered a pause for the construction of tracks over which mules could bring supplies to each brigade sector. That done, he resumed the assault on 30 November, and it quickly became obvious that the first phase of the assault had actually been of benefit. Over firmer ground the Canadians were able to charge the German obstacles more effectively, gaining 1,000 yards before nightfall. The cost however, for the one day battle, had been 2,321 men."[75]

Instead of driving the remaining 1/4-mile, Currie "tried Haig's patience" by "insisting on a seven-day pause to reorganize his artillery and to bring forward and acclimatize the 1st and 2nd Divisions. By 06 November he was ready to proceed and at dawn that day launched the Canadian troops forward behind a tremendously powerful barrage. The troops covered so much ground that the German counter-fire fell behind them. Although the German defences held out stubbornly, they were finally overpowered at close quarters. The ridge fell within three hours. Although there was hardly a brick left standing in the pulverized village, the Canadians were able to look across the sombre plain towards the distant coast. To obtain this view, the Canadian Corps had suffered 15,654 casualties between 18 October and 14 November, almost exactly the number Currie had estimated the battle would cost."[76]

Casualties had forced the British forces to reduce the numbers of battalions in each of their infantry brigades. "The Canadian Corps resisted British pressure to do the same," believing it would break up an efficient fighting machine. Instead, "each of the existing battalions in the Canadian Corps was augmented by 100 men. Without any increase in staff or services, this gave each Canadian division more firepower and 1,200 more men in the line. The 5th Canadian Division, then still in England, was broken up for the immediate augmentation of the four divisions in France. Its artillery, however, fought with the Canadian Corps."[77]

The Canadians held Lens and Vimy Ridge during the major German spring offensives, except for "the 2nd Division which fought with the British until July. Three Canadian divisions were therefore intact and rested when the initiative passed to the Allies in August."[78]

Walter's diary records the following observations on his experiences at Passchendaele.

October 31st
Moved to Vlamertinge, Belgium. Camped in open field in the mud.

November 1st
Guns went up the line through Ypres (Ieper). Out in the salient to a position south side of Weiltje road. Hard to find solid ground enough between shell holes to carry the guns.

November 2nd
Lots of action. Were strafed with gas during the night.

November 3rd
Bdr. Scott wounded. Moyer killed.

November 4th
Moved guns ahead 700 yards in front of Kier farm.

November 5th
Were shelled all day. Lot of casualties on plank road at left.

November 6th, 1917
Six hours strafe for Passchendaele.[79] Guns in the open front, and 4.5 Howitzer, back of us. Deaf as a post. Sent down line to wagon lines at Ouderdom road.

November 8th
   Jack O'Brian wounded.

November 9th
   Went up the line with Haddock. Built a little bivouac in mud.

November 10th
   Big strafe. Took Bert Tasker to dressing station. Elwood wounded. Rained all day. Terrible conditions at night. Lot of casualties, men and horses on plank road.

November 12th
   Kentish and Turner buried. Could not get back to guns for some time after carrying Turner to dressing station.

November 13th
   Went to wagon lines.

November 14th, 1917
   Went back up the line. Forward on working party. Helped repair plank road, 17th. Position shelled all day.

November 19th
   Caine and Bryan wounded. Helped carry Caine to the dressing station.

November 22nd
   Fritz seems to be angry. All forced to clear out. Joe Rankin jumped 18-foot trench. Whitehouse wounded at OP. Telephone pit blown in. Keebler wounded. Godfrey shell-shocked. Slightly shocked myself. On guard…feel kind of queer.

November 23rd

Guns moved ahead. Carried Murray Field to dressing station. Died later from loss of blood. A transfusion might have saved him. Corporal Webb lost a leg later. Corporal Debney and Sergeant O'Neal wounded.

November 24th

Carried Howard to dressing station. Eight days since a shave or a wash. Sent down the line.

November 25th, 1917

E Sub wheel team killed. Milson badly shaken up on a plank road. Battery moved forward to end of plank road. Abraham Heights.

November 27th

Allen Fraser killed. Milson wounded. Hart wounded, 28th.

November 29th

Attended Allen Fraser's funeral. Brandhock Military Cemetery. Corporal Rothwell, Bdr. Grant Smith killed. Bdr. Hughes, Signaler McCabe, McElroy and Mehan wounded.

November 30th

Sent up the line. Met Helman bringing the boys down. Victor Driver and I left the plank road and continued on #5 duck walk. Took cover in an old German tank until the barrage lifted.

Caught in the open during a heavy shelling, he and a friend name Vic who had been hit, climbed into an old German tank.[80] It sounded interesting to me, but he commented that:

"When Vic Dennis and I ducked into that German tank we didn't take much notice.[81] There were two dead Germans in it and they were ripe. We kept our head out a hole in the side of it until it was safe to go on. I carried Vic out to the hospital that afternoon. He died the next day from loss of blood".

German A7V tank from the Great War

December 1st
Took over B Sub gun. George Evans and Tom Balderson for crew.

December 2nd
Driver, Rawlings and Saunders badly wounded. Con. O'Neal and I reached Driver and Rawlings a little ahead of the next shell. Len Smith and Jack Spittal came running with the stretchers. I picked Driver up in my arms and ran ducking in and out of two shell holes when I was sure the next one was going down my neck. Reached plank road, winded. Shelling was so heavy we could not stop until we reached the dressing station. Doctor Barnett from Detroit had us carry them in. Jack Spittal and I stayed and helped him give first aid to get them ready for the ambulance. Saunders was wounded.

December 4th, 1917

At wagon lines at Ouderdom. Paid. Issued new uniform. Out exercising horses. Murrifield and Rawlings dead.

December 7th

Took rations up the line. Herb ball driving. Dugan killed. If a man volunteered for a dangerous duty or needlessly exposed himself, his comment was: "Brave men die young." He and I were appointed emergency stretcher-bearers for right section back at the Battle of Vimy. One day we decided that if our names were next on our sergeants' duty lists, to accept any duty, but to volunteer for nothing except for carrying out the wounded. Fritz got a direct hit on one of our machine-gun emplacements a little farther over Abraham Heights. One man crawled back to our guns badly wounded. Dugan immediately loaded him pick-a-back and started for the dressing station along the plank road. A whiz-bang killed Dugan. The wounded man crawled to the dressing station on his own power. Remembering Dugan through the years, I was always reminded of the last two lines of the poem *The Loss of the Prairie Bell*—"He did his duty, a dead sure thing, and Christ ain't going to be too hard on a man that has died for men".

December 8th, 1917

Stayed at guns to relieve Bennet. One stand to. Got gas back.

December 9th

Rained all day. Helped Sgt. Hanson's crew move C Sub gun from its inverted position in the left hole when it was blown up.

December 9th

Slightly wounded along right shoulder blade.

While I spoke with my grandfather about wounds and injuries, he discussed this incident that occurred while manhandling a gun during a move out of the Passchendaele salient.

"I was the man at the trail. I had the beam over my shoulder, hands on the grip side of trail with the spade between my legs, and several other men on the drag ropes. We felt the Woolly Bear coming. Everyone flopped in the mud, but I couldn't get out from under the trail quick enough, so tried to get most of me under the steel hat. I tried to get down a little and turned my head towards it. A piece of something gouged my right shoulder, tore my greatcoat down the back and ruined it. Ernie Bennett cleaned the wound out with iodine and applied the first field dressing".

"We then moved to Vimy town and dug in just off the road. The far end of the road was about four feet high. We built or dug a bivouac about 6 1/2 feet deep around it with steel rails and ties from a shot up railroad. An otter slide was set up at one side with a wet blanket to keep out gas. Fritz was shelling the road that night at about two minute intervals. We were standing by playing penny ante on a blanket on the floor of the dugout by candlelight. I said to George Haddock, "play my hand when the next one lands. I'll have time to go top side to take a leak and be back before the next one lands." He said "don't be a fool, use that old shell case behind you." I said, "the smell of that would kill the devil." I went up the slide and had just unbuttoned and turned on the tap when a big one struck the far side of the road. A chunk of mud about the size of a pail hit me right in the belly and knocked the wind out of me. I slid butt first into the dugout and flopped out on my back. Haddock says, "the dizzy bastard must be alive, he's still pissing." I didn't have enough wind left to argue the point."

December 10th
Started moving out. Stone wounded.

December 11th
Began manhandling guns down plank road 4:30 a.m. Waited for teams at end of double road. B Sub gun last in line. Sgt. Ede's teams had turned and I was hooking on the gun when Fritz opened up on the road with shrap. Needless to say, we came out of the Passchendaele salient at the gallop.

December 12th
Getting ready for trek back to France.

December 14th, 1917
Started south at daylight. Rode Aussie as coverer. Billeted at Strazeele.[82]

December 15th
Reached Gonneheim.[83]

December 16th
Reached Ohlain, France.

December 19th
Pay day.

December 21st
Rode Chubby through Bruay Bouchiers to hand over guns.

December 23rd
Leave to Auchel to visit Connor and Cooper. Got a ride in an army car through Camblain Châtelain to Houdain. Walked the rest of the way. Got back to Camblain in time for breakfast.

December 24th
Helped dress four pigs and a flock of geese for Christmas.

December 25th, 1917
Had a nice dinner in a school building in Ohlain. Had a few games of Euchre, with Thompson, Bennett and Price. Made rounds of Estaminets to see that the sleepy ones all got back to their blankets.

December 26th, 27th, 29th, 30th
Rested, went to baths.

December 31st
Moved up the road into huts.

January 1st, 1918
Sent to army school of mines for a course in deep dugout construction. Finished the course and returned to Ohlain on the 16th.

January 17th
Moved to Fort George in a blinding snowstorm. Rode Hungry Joe. Guns in a Brick Stack post.

January 20th
Up to guns with rations. Usual duties at wagon lines until the 5th.

February 5th, 1918
Took three G.S. wagons to Liévin for material, boards, plank, etc. Saw General Burstall.[84] He was examining officer when we of the old 10th Battery qualified our gun layers, 1912 and 1913 at Petawawa. Next few days, fixed hut, played penny ante, out to ride. To Liévin with working party. Haddock got back. Jock Bains went back to Canada. Mr. Edgecombe returned to Canada.

Here, I have to insert a very personal and to me the most interesting story Walter told me of the war. As a soldier in the present Canadian Army, it does not take long to appreciate that no matter which side you are on, the weather and terrain tend to be the same, only the enemy is different. Present times, politics and attitudes are affected by those who came before us in many strange ways. There are always two sides to a story, but because my grandfather Frederik Skaarup died before I knew him, I did not hear the stories from "the other side." He was living in the German occupied area of southern Denmark when the war came, having been conscripted into the German army in 1910, served two years compulsory service, and then went into the reserve mobilization force. He was recalled on mobilization, and therefore fought in the war in France and Belgium from day one in 1914.

Frederik C. Skaarup, 1914-1918

I was curious as to whether or not my two grandparents had fought in the same area, or perhaps been in the position where they might have been firing on each other. Because of our family tradition in the field of music, Gramp was able to tell me this incredible story about how he knew they had been the same place at the same time:

"I met your grandfather Skaarup about 1937 or 1938. They were living in River de Chute and bought the Hubbard's farm (next to ours). He and Harold came down with an old model Ford Tractor and ploughed out nearly half the farm.[85] (They) came back that winter and lumbered all winter. Fred came down with them, with a big gray team and hauled logs to Lakeville. I hardly saw any of them, they worked so hard. Harold would come down evenings and talk to Kathryn." [87]

"The next winter Mrs. Skaarup came down and we used to see each other quite often. I changed words with them quite often (while) threshing etc. There were no combines then. We often listened to him playing the trumpet on the verandah in the evenings. We discussed the war many times. One time in particular on 05 February 1918, I had charge of a team getting some lumber salvaged in an old blown up school. We heard a German Band playing the boys going out on relief in Lens just across no mans land from Liévin where we were. We checked the dates and your grandfather said that he may have been playing in that band".

"I have seen troops coming out of the line tired and dirty after a big push, make their first halt for a little rest. Sometimes a band would be waiting for them. Marching when not weary and with a good band will give some folks a tremendous thrill. But can you imagine a depleted unit coming out of the line from a hard position, tired, dirty, muddy and lousy, stumbling along just after dark, a few minutes halt just out of maximum gun range. "Fall in, quick march." Imagine that a band has been waiting for them, and what it would feel like as it begins playing "The British Grenadiers". The men would hunch their equipment up higher on their backs and their shoulders would straighten up. They would all have fallen in line four abreast without an order. No need for left-right. The muddy boots would seem to lighten up, and darned if the feet don't seem to get the beat of the music. They are old hands, and would soon disappear in the night. Your grandfather told me about playing the men out on the other side of the line in the same way".

February 19th
To Thelus to unveiling of monument. General Currie and all staff possible were there. General Currie gave the address.[88]

February 20th
Had a hard trip to Liévin for lumber. Fritz was bracketing the road in the Souchez valley.[89] We halted, dismounted close to a wall and a pile of rubble before crossing the Givenchy-en-Gohelle road. The next one struck behind the wall. The mules bolted. Everyone was able to mount, but Durham. He cleared the wheel and ran behind until we slowed up on the grade. Climbed into the back of the wagon out on the pole mounted.

February 21st, 1918
Took crew up on west side of Vimy Ridge, constructing reserve gun positions. Every night the flares showed the Germans were advancing both north and south of us. Generals' Currie, Haig and Stuart were on the ridge checking the situation. General Stuart looked over our work, February 28th.

March 2nd
General Stuart returned and gave us corrections for line of fire.

March 3rd
Finished gun pits, built a few bivvys for the men. Work discontinued as lines were holding.

March 7th
Attended funerals of Lieutenants Clark and Caffery, who were burned to death by exploding creolin and buffer oil at Ecuire. Up to guns as guide over light railway, 9th.

March 10th
Took Bob Thompson to Aubigny.

March 11th
Sent to Pernes on a machine-gun course.[90] Lectures and instruction on handling a Lewis gun, shooting over range. Returned 17th.

March 18th, 1918
Took working party up to left of Zivvy dump, digging reserve gun pits til the 21st.

March 20th
Up line with rations. Road shelled. Old Hungry got his wind up and bumped my nose with the top of his head.

March 22nd
Worked on reserve positions. Rode tall chestnut up on the ridge with Mr. Derry.

March 23rd
Rumours of big strafe. Standing by with teams. With working party til March 28th.

March 28th
Went with Sergeant Hanson scouting positions at Souchez. Came back over the Pimple.

March 29th
Up the line in charge of transport. Battery moved to front of the line. Had to dodge shells at Souchez corner. Later shelled at battery position. Came out through ruined village at the gallop.

My grandfather spoke of this period at some length. Through March 1918 trench mortar warfare increased. The Germans shot up flares that kept the line lit up for several minutes:

"We were standing by most of the time so BHQ had the battalion send up a man from each gun crew to help dig emplacements for the mortar boys. I was on several trips in no mans land with nothing for protection but our shovels. By the time you heard a pop from a flare pistol you had about three seconds to duck or be perfectly still until the flare burst over head. We had rations at the gun at 6 PM, and nothing more until returning to our guns just before daylight. Boy oh boy did a hard tack look and taste good."

"Except during a heavy strafe, our telegraphists kept communications between front line batteries, brigade headquarters, and Divisions. Big deals were handled from division, routine from brigade HQ."

"To make a night raid for information meant cutting our own wire or digging under, a sweet job in the night, crawling or running between flares to a listening distance. Enemy patrols played the same way. If two patrols contacted, the outfit that got one man to take back as a prisoner was very lucky. Everything was hand to hand and quiet. Most often both patrols would get back to their own lines and report enemy patrols on the alert. It took the monotony out of living on a quiet front."

I wondered how the guns were kept cool after all the rounds they fired, and about the size of the shell holes they made. He said that:

"We had canvas pails and poured water from shell holes down the muzzle of the gun after elevating the gun, it was easier that way. Shell holes were all sizes, some made to order from three feet across to any size about as deep as half the width."

March 31st, 1918
To Roelincourt with G.S. wagons. Took load of material to guns, Rode Bee back for orders.

April 2nd
Made trip to Souchez for mining equipment. Took it to the guns. Stayed there and took charge of crew digging deep dugout.

April 4th
Halderson upset the bread and tea ration into muddy trench. Did not hurt him much, but he got an awful cussing.

April 9th
Lee Bell got a slight wound in the knee.

April 12th
Handed over our guns and took over guns at red mill Château. Wagon lines moved to Boueflles. Remodeled round tower. Put ladder in round tower. Improvised speaking tube to officers quarters.

April 19th
Went on sniping gun crew at Whiz-Bang Corner.

April 20th, 1918
Got two Bosche with one shot.

April 21st
Shot up staff car away back. Fritz dropped some so close, destroyed our siege lamp. Relieved 25th.

April 26th
Back at Rouge Château. Repaired and extended light railway.

April 29th
Built bridge across Souchez River.

May 2nd
Muster parade. Ditched all surplus kit. All swimming in Souchez.

May 3rd
Weather beautiful.

May 4th
All sick. Fitzpatrick went to hospital.

May 5th, 1918
Inspected by R.F.A. General Sherry Davies kept his crew on their feet in A Sub, but when he got to B sub, I was so dizzy I could not see the barrage table and he discontinued the inspection. Spanish Influenza, only lasted about three days.

May 7th
Went forward at night to whisper position Liévin.

May 8th, 9th, and 10th
Very busy sniping. Moved sniping guns to Rabbit right of Liévin.

May 12th
Moved and took over guns from R.F.A. between Liévin and Calonne. Guns in the open…raining…made bivouac in a trench. Started digging a concealed position by railroad track, in front of Calonne.

May 16th
Took guns to position front of Liévin to calibrate. Stayed all night. Pit caught fire. Stopped the stories and songs for awhile.

May 17th, 1918
Calibrated gun. Moved back to position at night. Worked until morning, getting pit ready for the General to inspect. To swimming pool at Maroc on the 18th.

May 21st
Put in charge of a crew digging deep dugout under railroad.

May 23rd
With Wickens to Bully Grenay.

May 24th
To Calonne for timber.

May 25th
Went down the line with ration team for rest.

May 26th
Over to Sans-en-Gohelle to see the town.

May 27th
Sports day at Fosse (in SE Belgium). 10 Anchormen on our tug-of-war team.

May 28th
Got inoculated. Played sick and slept all day.

May 30th, 1918
Up the line with rations. Late for parade.

May 31st
Rode Billy up the line with Sgt. O'Neal on Chubby. Sgt. O'Neal stayed up; Sgt. Davies rode Chubby back. We had a glorious race across some open country coming back.

June 1st
Late for parade. Had to straighten out some corrugated iron. The blacksmith needed to make bake sheets for the cook, for punishment. I took several sheets down the road where a steamroller was working; gave the driver a package of Oro Pasqualis cigarettes. Lined the sheets in single file and he drove back and over them a few times and did a better job than I could have with a ten pound sledge.

June 2nd
Down to Angiers to First Division sports meet.

June 3rd
Went up the line on dugout gang. Dobson wounded.

June 5th, 6th, 7th
(Dug a) passage down about 30 feet, surveying. With a field line, plumb line, tape line and telephone wire, dug another entrance from the other side of the embankment. General Morrison inspected the position on the 9th.[91]

June 10th, 11th, 12th, 1918
Getting the dug out well under way. One side ready for signaler.

June 13th
Haddock and I go to the wagon lines at Fosse Ten.

June 14th
Picked for brigade tug of war team.[92] Had a try out.

June 15th

Went to sports at Vaudreuil. Pulled machine gunners team over in six minutes.[93] Several on the team dropped out and heavier men from the 24th and 30th Batteries took their places.[94] Jack Young as coach.

June 17th, 1918

Pulled 3rd Division supply column team on our own ground, winning in four minutes.

June 18th

Went to Bovigny Wood.

June 19th

Went to Pernes, pulled 5th CDA in forenoon, winning.[95] Pulled CGA team in the afternoon and brought home the silver cup.[96]

June 20th

Training. Extra rations.

June 21st

Shell burst in the football field, eleven casualties.

June 23rd

32nd (Field Battery) ball team played 24th (Field Battery), (score 3-2).

June 24th, 25th, 26th, 1918

Daily workouts with the 45th Battalion team.[97] Out for long route march. Saw some of the new tanks on maneuvers. Pulled over the 46th team with three extra men.[98]

British and Canadian WWI Mk 1 tank

June 28th
Went to Pernes, pulled 49th Battalion team across the line in six minutes.[99] A long, long six minutes.

June 29th
Route march to Bovigny (SE Belgium). Over to Fosse 10 for mail on the 30th.

July 1st
Went to Corps sports meet at Tincques. R.L. Borden spoke from the Grandstand.[100] 29th Battalion team pulled us across the line in four minutes.[101]

July 2nd, 1918
Vacation over, returned to battery.

July 3rd
Up the line with rations.

July 4th
In charge of street cleaning gang.

July 5th
Out to Bovigny section for maneuvers.

July 7th
Over to Sans-en-Gohelle, Fritz plane brought down in front of town.

July 9th
Football team played 43rd Battery team, thirteen to nothing.

July 11th
Team played 30th Field Battery team, two to one.

July 12th
Went up to guns at Calonne.

July 13th, 1918
Left section, moved back on Vimy Ridge, left of Zivvy dump.

July 14th
Moved to lines in front of Berthonval near old position, (April 1916).

July 15th, 16th, 17th
Usual routine.

July 18th
Up to Zivvy for gun. All guns came out at 2:00 a.m. Moved battery to Semincourt.[102]

July 19th
Guns went up the line. Went up in charge of transport. Shelled at right of Arras.

July 20th, 21st
At lines. Quiet. Exercise ride. Milked the cows for Madame.

July 22nd
Moved lines to Arras-St. Pol road near Louez.

July 23rd, 1918
With Mr. Wilson and other No. 1's, learning roads and streets of Arras. McElroy wounded.

July 24th
Over to Madagascar with G.S. wagons for lumber.

July 26th
In to Arras for a load of brick.

July 27th
To Maroueil to canteen.[103]

Amiens
The official war record continues to tell the story. Haig prepared a plan for an attack "north of the River Luce" in mid-July. "Marshall Foch approved the plan and placed the First French Army at Haig's disposal to act on the right of Rawlinson's Fourth Army, which was to be reinforced by the Canadian Corps." This battle would differ greatly "from the methods used by the British at the Somme and Passchendaele, in that they now sought to achieve surprise. There would be no preparatory bombardment to warn the enemy (in fact,

the heavy artillery fired without registration); massed tanks would be used instead."[104]

Rawlinson brought in "420 tanks, nine infantry divisions, three cavalry divisions and 2,080 guns." The British took serious measures "to conceal the presence of the Canadians" as the Germans considered their presence to be a likely indicator of an impending attack. They therefore were not moved into the front line until just before the assault. The Germans had only ten under-strength divisions in the line and four in reserve, and had not had time to construct strong defences. The frontage of the Allied attack "was some 14 miles, with the French advancing in the southern half. The Fourth Army was to assault with two corps, the Canadians on the right and the Australians on the left, while the British 3rd Corps would act as flank-guard on the Australian left."[105]

"An hour before dawn on 08 August 1918, British tanks lumbered forward through a heavy ground mist, the noise from their tracks a deafening sound" to the waiting soldiers, who were concerned that "an enemy bombardment would wreak havoc in the crowded assembly areas." The British and Dominion guns however, suddenly crashed with one voice along the front. The surprise was complete. The German "front dissolved in panic and confusion, as tanks and infantry tore through their positions." The attack swept inexorably forward, with "the main resistance encountered coming from pockets of infantry or machine-gun posts which often capitulated when outflanked. For the first time in the war, massed cavalry, accompanied by light "whippet" tanks, came forward to exploit success. On the 4th Divisions front however, thickly emplaced machine-guns swept the flat fields and the Canadian infantry were forced to dig in short of their objective. Elsewhere, the day's objectives had all been reached and a firm grip obtained on the Amiens Outer Defence Line across the entire Corps front."[106]

"On the Canadian front the German line had been thrown back eight miles, while the Australians had advanced seven miles, the French five and the British two. Fourth Army's casualties had been about 9,000, but the Germans had lost 27,000 men, 400 guns and large numbers of mortars and machine-guns. The Canadian Corps had captured 5,033 prisoners and 161 guns at a cost of some 4,000 casualties. Many of the German batteries had been overrun before they had fired more than a few rounds. Greater than the material loss was the moral effect on the German Army." Amiens would later be described by historians as "the decisive engagement of the First World War."[107]

Walter recorded the events as follows.

July 28th
Up the line to position east of Arras and Cambrai road with GS wagon to bring down cooks and signalers equipment, preparing to move.[108]

July 29th
Guns came out of action.

July 30th, 1918
Marched to Aubigny-en-Artois.[109] Entrained for Amiens front.

July 31st
Detrained at Salouël, south of Amiens in the early morning. Marched to Cagny. Slept all day in the deserted houses. Had a swim in the Arve.

August 1st
Moved from Cagny to Bovs Wood. Slept under the stars.

August 2nd
Raining. Moved farther back in the wood to old French lines

August 3rd

Wood full of Americans, Australians and Canadian Corps. Guns go into action in wood near Villers-Bretonneux.[110] Moved wagon lines to rear of wood. Drove big gray team on G.S. wagon all day. Up the line at night. Enemy hostile. Played groundhog.

August 5th, 1918

Orders to sleep during the day. Mashed potatoes and roast beef for dinner. In charge of B. Sub gun. Right section started to move. A. Sub got in a shell hole in the dark and broke the pole at Gentilles. Got into position in front of wood at daybreak.

August 6th

Concealed gun under an apple tree, Fitzpatrick and I roll up in a tarpaulin and slept all day. Go to Gentilles cross road at night to guide other five guns in. Was shelled going out. But was quiet when we brought guns in and covered them with camouflage before daylight.

August 7th

Slept during the day. Worked all night getting guns in position in the open in front of the wood. Ammunition ready and funk holes dug.

August 8th

Start of big push on the Amiens front. Strafe started 4:00 a.m. Heavy fog hid our position, 8:00 a.m., stood down enemy out of range. Prisoners coming steadily. Went ahead in afternoon. Bivouacked near Hangard.

August 9th, 1918

Enemy still retreating. Moved ahead again near Le Quesnel.[111] Standing by guns all day.

August 10th
Stood by all day. Milson and Smart wounded. Lost three horses.

August 11th
Dysentery hit us. Took Haddock to hospital. Moved horses into wood. In charge of vehicles. Moved guns and lines ahead near Folies. Brigade attached to 4th Division for a time.

The Hindenburg Line
From here the official war record continues. "Although the Battle of Amiens continued until 11 August, only another three miles were gained. By then the Germans had rushed up 18 divisions; British tank power had dwindled through mechanical failure and enemy action; and more seriously, the attacking troops had come up against the formidable trench lines of the old Somme battleground of 1916. Largely at the instigation of General Currie, Haig broke off the battle in favour of three new thrusts: the Third Army would attack towards Bapaume; the First Army would strike south-east from the Arras sector; and the Fourth Army would exploit any withdrawal from the Somme. The Canadian Corps would fight as part of Horne's First Army."[112]

"Horne's task was to force the defences that screened the flank of the Hindenburg Line facing Arras. He was then to break the hinge of the Hindenburg system and, swinging southward, to deny those defences to the enemy falling back before the Third Army. The line of Horne's advance would be directly on Cambrai, the hub of the German defence system on the British front. The German positions facing the First Army were sited in depth and extremely strong. Immediately in front, in the vicinity of Monchy-le-Preux, were the old British trenches lost in March 1918. Behind this again was the former German front line. Two miles to the east lay another system, the Fresnes-Rouvroy line. A mile farther east, the Droucourt-Quéant Switch provided a terribly strong and deep system of trenches with concrete shelters and heavy wire designed to block any advance into the Douai plain. Like the Hindenburg Line, of which it was an extension, the D-Q Line had been under construction for almost two years and was considered absolutely impregnable. Between that and Cambrai, the Canal du Nord formed a major obstacle."[113]

"The task of breaking these defences was given to the Canadians with the 17th British Corps cooperating on their right. It was a tough assignment, calling for successive frontal assaults against a desperately resisting enemy. The battle began on 26 August. By nightfall Monchy and the ground 1000 yards beyond it (including both the old British and German trench lines) was in Canadian hands. The Fresnes-Rouvroy Line, the objective for the 27th, was not reached that day; not before the 30th, after bitter fighting, was the line fully pierced. Currie, appreciating the formidable nature of the D-Q Line, the next objective, obtained Horne's permission to postpone his attack until 02 September when his preparations would be ready. These consisted of powerful artillery support and tanks to roll paths through the belts of wire which were too dense for the preliminary bombardment to cut completely."[114]

"At dawn on the 2nd, behind a heavy barrage, the infantry went forward. Heavy tanks clawed through the wire that remained, snapping the strands like cotton. The infantry's task, although stern enough, proved lighter than had been expected. German morale was cracking, and although some fiercely defiant pockets fought stubbornly to the end, there was little resistance elsewhere along the front. The enemy surrendered in large numbers, and that night the Germans pulled back. Nothing now remained between the captured D-Q Line and the west bank of the Canal du Nord."[115]

"In fact, the Germans felt themselves compelled to withdraw behind the Hindenburg defences and, indeed, all along the front as far south as the Aisne and also in Flanders. They relinquished the whole of the gains of the March offensive and also most of those of the April offensive in Flanders. On 03 September Marshal Foch outlined his plans for the

Allied campaign on the Western Front. Three British armies, the First, Third and Fourth, were either facing the Canal du Nord or approaching the Hindenburg Line. To prevent the enemy massing all his reserves against them, Foch determined on a general offensive all along the front. Four great blows would be struck, first, by the three British armies against Cambrai and St. Quentin; second, by the French centre beyond the Aisne; third, in the St.Mihiel Salient, by American forces who would later combine with the French in a drive towards Mézières; and finally, by the British and Belgians in the north, who would drive towards Ghent and Bruges. For the Canadian Corps there would be a pause to permit the British farther south to reach the Hindenburg Line."[116]

"Meanwhile, Currie studied the ground. He concluded that a frontal attack on the Canal du Nord would be unsound because of the nature of the obstacle, as the ground was flooded, the canal itself would be difficult to cross under fire, and there were successive defences from which any advance to the east would more dangerously enfiladed the deeper it went. To the south, on the other hand, a 4,000-yard stretch of the canal had not been completed; this was dry and the excavated bed ran between higher and firmer ground. He proposed to take advantage of the dry portion of the canal by having the corps boundary extended 2,600 yards to the south. Through this one-and-a-half mile funnel Currie would pass 50,000 men, guns, tanks and transport and, after reaching the far bank, would spread them out fanwise in a 10,000-yard arc to the north and east. It was a daring concept, calling for skillful leadership and strict discipline. If the enemy artillery should become aware of the congestion in the narrow avenue of assault, the resulting slaughter would virtually destroy the Corps. Yet against that risk was the certainty of extremely heavy casualties in a frontal assault, still without assurance of success. With some misgivings, Horne approved Currie's plan."[117]

"On 15 September, Haig confirmed his intentions. The First and Third Armies would operate jointly towards Cambrai, with Horne seizing the great defensive feature of Bourlon Wood, while Byng advanced on the city itself. The Canadian Corps, with the 11th British Division under command, would take the wood and then establish a front along the Sensée Canal, north of Cambrai. The preliminary obstacle, the Canal du Nord, would be crossed on 27 September."[118]

"In the dusk of the evening of 26 September, the Canadians moved forward. By midnight they were assembled opposite the dry section of the canal, huddled together for warmth, and for the most part in the open. The night wore on, and as yet there was no evidence of enemy counter-preparation. Suddenly, as the eastern sky was brightening, the opening barrage flashed out, shocking the men to action. Before the Germans could retaliate, the initial waves had crossed the canal and were fanning out from the bridgehead. Nevertheless, the follow-up troops suffered casualties as the Germans, now aware of their danger, subjected the bed of the canal to a violent bombardment. The results of the first day justified Curries generalship. His calculated gamble had given him the canal du Nord at relatively light cost. More than hat, Bourlon Wood, the essential objective, had also fallen."[119]

"Thereafter, the Germans, sensitive to the threatened loss of Cambrai and the railways converging on it, poured in reinforcements. The German strength facing the Corps grew from four divisions on 27 September to ten by 01 October, together with 13 special machine-gun companies, which could offer grim resistance under conditions of open warfare. Progress was costly and slow. On the night of 01 October Currie broke off the action because of the exhaustion of his troops. Yet, although it was not immediately apparent, the Canadian thrust, combined with those by the Third and Fourth Armies farther south, had so exhausted German reserves that the enemy was no longer capable of serious resistance."[120]

"When the assault was resumed on the night of 8-9 October, it caught the enemy preparing to withdraw. Canadian troops entered Cambrai with ease and by 11 October had pushed on some six miles beyond the city. Since 26 August, the Corps had fought its way forward

23 miles through the main German defensive system which had been manned in turn by 31 identified divisions. The Canadians had suffered nearly 31,000 casualties in the six-week period, but German losses, (never published), included 18,585 prisoners, as well as 371 guns and nearly 2,000 machine guns."[121]

"On 12 September, the First U.S. Army, fighting its first large battle at St. Mihiel, caught the Germans in a withdrawal and straightened out the salient. On 26 September, in conjunction with the French, the Americans opened the Meuse- Argonne battle on the British right. While this did not succeed in drawing off reserves from in front of Haig's three armies until the Hindenburg Line had been broken, it did gain seven miles and eventually caused the Germans to move troops farther south."[122]

"The flank protection afforded by the Canadian Corps enabled the third British Army immediately to the south to breach the Hindenburg Line south-west of Cambrai on 27 September. The Fourth Army, south of the Third, opened a powerful attack two days later; in an impressive display of strength it bored through the Hindenburg defences north of St. Quentin and burst into the open country three miles beyond. The previous day, the Second British Army and the Belgians had advanced in Flanders, recovered Messines and Passchendaele and gained nine miles before being halted by the condition of the ground."[123]

"Behind the German Army, which was still fighting stubborn rearguard actions, the German nation and its allies fell apart. In September, the final British offensive in Palestine tore the Turks to pieces. An offensive in the Salonika Theatre succeeded against the Bulgarians, and at the end of September Bulgaria capitulated. On 04 October the German and Austrian governments dispatched notes to President Wilson asking for armistice negotiations."[124]

Walter's comments on this period are recorded as follows.

August 13th
Guns move forward in direction of Vipers wood.

August 14th
To Marquivillers to ammunition dump.[125]

Aug 15th
Ammunition very scarce. Sent on Chubby to watch for the arrival of ammunition lorries. Place was shelled. I got Chubby into a trench back just above the top. A splinter tore through his neck. Got his bridle and saddle off before he fell. Loaded the works on my back and cleared out.

August 16th, 1918
Kitchener wounded.

August 18th
Moved lines to valley to the rear of Vrély.[126] Guns to position in front of Vrély. Ennannaam and Whittle wounded.

August 19th
At lines.

August 20th
Up the line looking out roads. Up with water cart at night.

August 22nd
Up the line in the evening.

August 23rd
Over to Caix to baths.[127]

August 24th
Up the line with transport. Guns come out, all move to old camp lines near Hangard. Heavy electric storm, killing several mules in 43rd.

August 25th
Rode ahead with advance party, through Villers-Bretoneaux, [128] Toutencourt, Corbie[129] and located billets for battery at Hérissart.[130]

August 26th
On advance again through Pas.[131] Bivouacked battery (nearby) at Warlincourt-les-Pas.

August 27th
Rode with advance to Habarcq.[132] 2nd Division went over in front of Arras. Going strong, so move on to old No Man's Land, in front of Arras and bivouacked for the night.

August 28th, 1918
On guard. Guns moved forward ahead of Monchy-le-Preux.[133]

August 29th and 30th
Quiet.

August 31st
Brewerton and Young wounded. Boys get an armload of parcels from home. Big feed. Fitzpatrick sick in the morning.

September 1st
Moved guns forward. Worked about all night. Were shelled heavily with H.E. and gas. Labey, Davies, Roll, Manly, Pokin, Horn and Perdu wounded and Letty killed. Smith gassed. Whirled bandages on several

R.F.A. Helped Bennett and O'Neal fix up some bad cases. Lost some good horses.

September 2nd

Strafe started 5.00 a.m. Runcini, Cox, Macle, Dubs, Soden and Heney killed. Helman and Shultz wounded, Shultz the forth time. Six horses killed. Moved forward in front of Remy.[134] Slept in shell holes, when gas was not too thick.

September 3rd, 1918

Not feeling too good. Guess I sniffed too much gas. Explored some deep German dug outs, side of sunken road. German machine gunners had made a last minute stand until one of our Highland regiments and a whippet tank annihilated them. Greatest number of dead in a small area I encountered during the war.

Whippet Tank

September 4th
Uneventful.

September 5th
Stayed in position near Remy as reserve battery until night. Moved guns back to wagon lines. Lot of stuff coming over.

September 7th
Rested. Lot of the boys went in to town and celebrated.

September 8th
Moved to Saint-Quentin for rest.

September 9th
Made a harness room. Bennett and I built a little bivouac back of the Gun Park. Really some home. Bob Thompson found an abundance of mushrooms growing between the rows in a turnip field. Salvaged all he could in his steel hat. Went back, crawled along a ditch to the end of a guarded potato field. Confiscated about a dozen new potatoes. Earnie borrowed a dixie lid with some bacon grease in it. I built a fire. Promoted Bob to cook. I helped peel the mushrooms and slice the potatoes, along with our bread, tea and scouse, we had a banquet fit for Marshall Foch.

September 12th, 1918
In town with Bennett for a feed of eggs and chips. Next week, maneuvers, exercise rides, etc.

September 19th
Took gun to Achicourt to mobile workshops.[135]

September 21st
Encore eggs and chips with Bennett.

September 22nd
Paid. Up at 2:45 a.m. Moved in front of Cherisy.[136]

September 23rd
Guns gone to be calibrated.

September 24th, 1918
Centre section went into action.

September 25th
All guns moved to an old German position in front of Pronville[137] and left of Inchy-en-Artois.

September 26th
Up the line with transport. Ran into a few shells at cookhouse Rode Bennet's horse, Chum. Returning, met wagon lines moving ahead to Pronville.

September 27th
Strafe started at daylight. Stood down. Stopped long enough to feed and moved ahead across Canal du Nord. Dry crossing.

September 28th
Moved guns ahead of Bourlon.[138] Watered horses in an open reservoir in the back of the village. First water in thirty-six hours. Some of the horses could not be held and plunged in over their backs. Drivers wading ashore. Ferrier quite uneasy, but no sick horses. Major Burns killed at OP. Signaler Berry had two German prisoners carry his body back to lines.

September 29th, 1918
Up at 4:30 a.m. Moved guns ahead to side of slope back of Saint-Ole [Aubin or Remy?] and Cambrai.

September 30th
Buried Major Burns. Sgt. Matthews and Smith killed. Guns moved ahead nearer Saint Ole.

October 1st
Moved wagon lines to rear of Raillencourt.[139] McDade and Allen wounded. Stood by guns with teams from 12 Midnight until morning.

October 2nd
SOS at dusk. Hurried stand too with the horses. False alarm. Lines move back to Bourlon Wood. Wickens rode Hungry Joe to guns on orderly duty. Ran into Shrapnel. Hungry Joe was game to the last. Carried him back to the lines before he dropped.

I spoke to my grandfather about this incident. He confirmed that Wickens had been riding Hungry Joe out to the guns while on orderly duty, but ran into heavy shrapnel.[140] Hungry Joe was hit with a shell splinter, but was "game to the last," and in spite of the wound the horse carried Wickens back to the safety of the battery lines before dying.[141]

October 3rd
With gun teams to forward lines near Raillencourt.

October 4th
Rode to baths. Shelled on way back.

October 6th, 1918
Went to Agnez-les-Duisans on anti gas course.[142] Classes. Lectures. Polish and shine. Met Ellis McLeod. Went to cinema, saw, "Under Two Flags." Lived through sham mustard gas attack, etc.

October 12th

Started back up the line through Arras, Bourlon. Stayed the night at 2nd. DC. Went to Raillencourt. Oliver Eastman was there trying to locate the unit. We stayed in an old house in St. Ole. Were directed to 8th Brigade in action at Naves[143] in front of Cambrai. We found, not 8th Brigade Artillery, but 8th Brigade Infantry[144] holding against a severe counter attack. We retreated at the double to Cambrai. Received directions at General Burstall's H.Q.[145]

October 14th

Reached lines at Baralle, guns at Epinoy.[146]

October 15th, 1918

8th Brigade buried General Lipsett at Queant.[147]

Pursuit to Mons

The official war record states that "on 16 October 1918, with the Hindenburg Line broken and Cambrai lost, Ludendorff ordered his troops back to the Hermann Line. Part of this was based northeast of Cambrai on the Escaut (Scheldt) River in the neighbourhood of Valenciennes. The Canadians crossed the Sensée Canal on the 17th and pushed out cavalry and armoured cars to maintain contact with the retreating Germans. This phase of the war was extremely exhilarating for the Corps. Demolitions could be heard as the Germans systematically cratered roads and destroyed bridges, but there was a strange absence of gunfire. Bands played as battalions marched through liberated towns and villages to the acclaim of French civilians who proffered wine and coffee and bedecked the men with flowers."[148]

"On the 20th however, the Germans began to show their teeth. There was some long-range shelling and roadblocks were now being covered by fire. Resistance stiffened during the next two days. The Canadians were approaching Valenciennes and it became obvious the enemy was about to stand and fight. The Corps paused along the Escaut Canal until the rest of the First Army came into line. As a key point in the Hermann Line, Valenciennes had been well chosen. The Canal de L'Escaut, covered by trenches and wire, barred approach from the west, southwest and north had been extensively flooded. The only dry approaches lay to the east and south, and these were dominated by a heavily defended hill, Mont Houy. Five German divisions held Valenciennes, and three of them were concentrated on or near Mont Houy. On 28 October, a British attack took the hill but could not hold it; the British had to be satisfied with part of the southern slope. Thereafter this objective was entrusted to the Canadian Corps."[149]

"The Canadian attack on 01 November was completely successful, due mainly to massive artillery support. Working to a carefully coordinated program, the guns poured a torrent of shells on the German positions. In all, about 2,140 tons of explosives were fired, almost as much as had been expended by both sides in the entire South African War. The result was that a single infantry brigade overran Mont Houy, taking nearly 1,800 prisoners. That night the Germans retreated from Valenciennes and abandoned the Hindenburg Line. The advance swept on."[150]

The Germans were now retreating "from Verdun to the sea before relentless Allied pressure. For a month now, armistice negotiations had been in progress, with the Allied terms stiffening as the extent of German demoralization became more and more apparent. On 24 October a final note from President Wilson abandoned the concept of a negotiated armistice for what was virtually unconditional surrender. On 10 November the Canadian Corps reached the outskirts of Mons, the scene of the first engagement between British and German troops in 1914. That night, the town changed hands without a struggle."[151]

"On 11 November, at eleven o'clock in the morning, the hostilities ended and the sound of firing ceased. Wild enthusiasm marked the occasion in every Allied city, but within the Corps there were no elated scenes. It would take time to adjust and grope for thoughts of home. What the future would bring to the men and to Canada was uncertain, but, both for good and ill, the old, pre-war world had disappeared forever."[152]

"At Mons the Canadians learned that they were to march to the Rhineland as part of Plumer's Second Army, the British Army of Occupation. Sir Arthur Currie received the news with gratification as an honour his Corps had well earned. Two Canadian divisions formed a sixth of the total occupation force. On the morning of 04 December the leading units reached the German frontier, but crossing of the Rhine at Cologne and Bonn nine days later was considered more significant. Plumer took the salute at the Cologne crossing, and at Bonn the distinction was accorded to Sir Arthur Currie."[153]

Walter's records for this same period unfold as follows.

October 17th
Went to the guns at Epinoy.

October 18th
Guns move forward to Aubigny-au Bac. Wagon lines to Epinoy. Crossed canal on a pontoon bridge. Gun teams crossed. The mules on the ammunition wagons, especially old Teddy, refused. A lead team of horses from each gun was hooked on ahead of each mule team and they crossed without trouble. Picked up a German 9mm Luger, that I was lucky enough to get home as a souvenir.[154]

October 19th
Battery changed fronts. Started pushing north in the last big push of the war. Bosche on the run. 36 hour march through Aniche[155] and stopped next night at Fenain.[156]

October 20th, 1918
Moved ahead to Hornaing.[157] Guns at Hélesmes. McFarlane wounded.

October 21st
Leave warrant in. New uniform. Started with Scorn for Paris. Walked, ran and jumped lorries to Arras. With four RCR boys,[158] stole a hitch in an empty boxcar, planning to jump it at St. Pol and catch the 11:00 PM leave train. We closed the door, lay down and kept quiet til the guard passed. All went to sleep, not waking until the train stopped at Maroeuil. Had to go back to Etapes Rouen, leaving at 9:30 p.m. 23rd.

October 23rd, 1918
Arrived in Paris.

October 24th
Breakfast at the Canadian Club Hotel de Iena. Roamed the city with a bunch of Americans, learning to navigate the Metropole and trying not to let the world pass us by.

October 25th
Slept til noon. Went to the Army and Navy leave club. Paid for a double room for the rest of our leave. Attended a Club Ball in the evening. VADS Guides, Red Cross personnel, all good dancers.

October 26th, 1918
Visited Senate House, Notre Dame Cathedral, forenoon. To Luna Park in the afternoon. Follies Bergere in the evening. Shirley Kellogg sang "Scotland Forever."

October 27th
Went on steamer ship up the Seine 15 miles to St. Cloud. To English Theatre in evening. Saw General Post.

October 28th
Went to cinema in afternoon. To club ball in the evening.

October 29th

Dinner at CYMCA. Saw COO EEs in afternoon. Whist party in the evening.

October 30th

Riding with **Amy Johnson** through bridle paths in the Bois-de-Bologne.[159] To concert at club in the evening.

Walter is on the first horse to the left in the picture, Amy, who later became a famous Aviatrix is sixth from the left.

October 31st

To Gaumont Picture Palace in afternoon. Club dance in evening.

November 1st, 1918

Dinner at Hotel de Iena. Out to Versailles through grounds Marble Palace, the statues and paintings from the time of Louis XIV. Went to Casino de Paris in the evening.

November 2nd
Raining. Explored some of the large department stores. To Royal Horse Guards concert in the evening.

November 3rd
To British Embassy church in the morning. Visited Les Invalides, (Napoleon's) Trophies of French wars, armouries, and relics from St. Helena. Up in the big wheel. To Gaumont pictures in the evening.

November 4th
Visited Corner of Slighty. To club dance in the evening.

November 5th
Visited wax works Le Musée Grevin. Club dance in the evening.

November 6th
Rained all day. Slept. To Alhambra Theatre in the evening.

November 7th, 1918
Rumours of an armistice. Start back up the line. Reach Rouen rest camp. Went to leave details camp for a day. Entrained and arrived at Etapes, morning of the 9th. Reached Somain. Stayed the night at staging camp.

November 10th
Went through Denain and stayed the night at Valenciennes staging camp.

In between the early series of letters my Grandfather Walter and I exchanged, I had been attending Vocational Schools in Gander and Grand Falls, Newfoundland. For my third year, I moved from Grand Falls to St John's, Newfoundland, where I attended the College of Trades and Technology. While there one of my roommates invited me to join the Militia in the fall of 1970. I was taken-on-strength (TOS) with the 56th Field Squadron, Royal Canadian Engineers (RCE), at Pleasantville, Newfoundland, on 22 February 1971. My lady at that time held a lot of interest, and I may not have written many letters. After graduating in June 1971, I went to Nova Scotia, then New Brunswick, and later to Toronto, Ontario for part of the summer, before going back to school at the Nova Scotia College of Art and Design (NSCAD) in Halifax in September 1971. I was also fortunate enough to get into residence at the University of Kings College. There were no Militia engineers in Halifax, so I joined 723 Communications Squadron, Royal Canadian Signal Corps, and was TOS in time to participate in my first November 11th parade. This of course prompted me to write to Gramp to ask him about what it was like on that historic day.

November 11th

Started early. Met the people that had evacuated before the line of battle, returning to their homes. Women hauling farm wagons with bedding, cooking utensils, old women and babies on top. Dog carts, goat carts, women leading children by the hand. Babies in arms…all cold…many crying. I had my haversack available space filled with chocolate bars to treat the boys. Broke them in pieces and passed them to passing children. Gave half a bar to a young girl trying to soothe a crying baby at a very empty looking breast as she trudged along and nearly got mobbed. Reached the battery 10:40, just 20 minutes before the cease-fire. Detailed to advance party from Jamappes. Rode through city of Mons. Flags flying. People waving, shouting Vive le Canadiennes. A Provost Captain halted us with the information that the stretch was being cleared for General Currie and staff's triumphant entry into the square, and for us to detour, tout de goddam suit. Most of the boys had a girl in the saddle with them and nobody was insulted. We rode through Mons to the adjoining town of Nimy.[160] We were shown where the different batteries would go into position, and streets to billet the men. Inspected the houses, marked with chalk on the doors, or gatepost number that could be accommodated. Joined the party. Returned to Jemappes and guided 43rd Battery to their lines, gun position and billets. 32nd Battery had been guided in to right front of Nisy where the Belgian army had put up such a desperate resistance to the invading Germans in 1914.

My favourite story of the war that he told me is about his experience the day the war ended. He was sent through Mons on 11 November 1918, and passed General Currie and a platoon of Lancers lined up for the triumphant entry into the city.

"There were five of us on the long track going through to Nerring to arrange billets for the Eighth Brigade. The military police headed us off at the square, and shunted us through another part of the city. Before we had progressed very far, everyone had a girl on horseback with him. I followed my good resolution until we passed the hospital. A busty looking woman came running down the steps. I gigged the sorrel to the sidewall, pulled my foot from the stirrup. "Ascendez Mademoiselle". "Mon Monsieur, j' allez a l' apothecarie. Viens tout de suit." I slipped to the back of the old universal saddle and she came up sideways. I promptly took her in my arms. I was enjoying a hug that smelled like chloroform, until she slipped off and went into the drug store saying "merci pour le souvenirs." She had snipped every button but the top two off my overcoat while I was enjoying myself."

November 12th
Took transport to Jemappes through Mons, Belgium, loaded with kids singing 'Le Barbanconne, Le Marsellaise. More shouting than singing.

November 14th
Billeted in houses with Belgian people. I often think of the widow Le Grand in her little house on the hill. She showed Earnie Bennett and I her best room, bare of furniture, which we promptly took over and spread our blankets on the floor. That night we got an extra ladle of tea

and poured her cup full. The next day found our blankets spread on a nice bed of straw. The next day we jockeyed for position in line to get the heel of the loaf because they were thicker and shared with her. The next day she put milk in our tea, the source of supply a mystery to us. Later, one early morning in a bushy pasture over the hill, a large ewe was discovered standing on a box eating some vegetable scrap, from which madam obtained a bowl full of milk.

November 27th, 1918
In Mons, saw King Albert of Belgium as he passed through the square.

November 30th
Saw the Dumbbells concert party in HMS Pinafore.

December 5th
Went with Walter Tees, Frank Gourlay and Oliver Eastman by train to Brussels on weekend leave. Over the weekend, the engineers had repaired the east and west railroads and discontinued the north and south service. We had to walk back to Mons, reaching there December 11th. To tell of the fun and happenings on that trip would fill a book.

December 11th
Battery moved to Breceniques.

December 12th, 1918
Battery moved to Famillereaux. Civilians invited us to a dance. My partner for the evening, Lea Paradene, 5 feet 10 and beautiful.

December 14th
Battery moved to Grez Doiceau.

December 18th
Battery moved to Gastouche and stayed there the winter.

Post script from the official war records.
"In the First World War the Canadian Corps achieved a reputation unsurpassed in the Allied armies. After the Somme, its record had been one of unbroken victory. It emerged successfully from every test, no matter how severe, and its professional ability had proved second to none. Canada had begun the war with little military experience and with practically nothing in the way of a standing army. She ended it with a superb fighting machine; "the greatest national achievement of the Canadian people since the Dominion came into being." A total of 619,636 men and women served in the Canadian Army in the First World War and of these 59,544 gave their lives and another 172,950 were wounded. That such a war record would carry Canada to full autonomy had been foreseen by Sir Robert Borden, and so it proved. A separate Canadian signature on the Peace Treaty signified that the status of nationhood had been achieved."[161]

A family visit to Vimy in 1960.

Walter's closing diary entries are as follows.

February-March 1919

Late in February, moved to Le Harve. In March, moved to Whitley camp in England. Took long leave to Ireland, crossed the Irish sea from Holly Head to Kingstown. Went to Dublin. Too many discharged soldiers still wearing khaki thronging the streets, so went to Belfast. Not much better there. Sgt. Brennan had given me a letter of introduction and address of relatives living between Magherafelt and Coolshinny so went there. Such hospitality could not be excelled. The neighbours called and invited me to their homes. The Wileys, the Palmers, the Stewards and others, whom I did not have time to visit. I walked the hills with the young people. Climbed Slevegallon Mountain. Could see into three countries, also, Loch Neagh to the north. Bannwater to the south, and Giants Causeway to the northeast. Where the road we returned by met the main road, there were broad turns to the right and left, leaving a three cornered grassed over space. This was Margaret's grave, buried about a hundred years ago. The legend, she was a witch and feared by the people, lived alone and cursed everyone that came near her. When she was found dead she was not allowed a lot in the cemetery, so a grave was dug here 100 feet deep and she was buried face down, so, if per chance, she decided to go places she would go in a hotter direction.

Came back to Belfast. Toured the city with some relatives of the Wileys. Caught the Fleetwood boat from Belfast back to England. Took the train to Liverpool and London. Made contact with my old friend, Sam Price. We bought a camera and hardly slept the next four days seeing the city. When we returned to Whitley, the brigade had sailed. We were transferred to Ripon. I can only describe our stay there as a wonderful holiday. Bounds 15 miles in any direction. We roamed the surrounding country. Played Crown and Anchor until one or the other of us won enough to buy a feed down town. Obtained extra clothing. Washed during the day and every second night, went to the Spa baths. One morning roll call, Sam's name was called and he was sent on his way rejoicing. Jack Young had been released from hospital and arrived at camp. We did a lot of boating on the Ripon river. Joined a picnic party one afternoon and Jack met the girl he later married. His first wife had passed away a year before, while in France.

May, 1919

About May 1st, transferred to Ryl camp in Wales. Met Harley Olmstead. Visited the grave of young McLean, a Woodstock boy that had died there. My only duty there: meet the train and guide any New Brunswick men to our section of the camp. Only one man, Sgt LeRoy Mooers, a boy I knew in high school 1907-1908 arrived.

May 15th

Embarked at Liverpool.

May 24th

Arrived in Halifax. Anchored in harbour to let the Acquatania dock first.

May 25th

Entrained, arriving in Saint John the morning of 26th.

May 26th, 1919

Sgt. Melvin Lawrence marched us to barracks mess hall, and we enjoyed our last army ration. We turned in our blankets, rubber sheet, gas mask, etc. Received our pay. Chase, Cogger, Adams, Diamond and I were given transportation to Woodstock, arriving there 11:00 p m.

That's all.

Postscript

I eventually in some of the letters I wrote to my Grandfather, I had to ask about how he and the women he met had gotten along. I had introduced him to my girlfriend, (now my very beautiful wife), and asked him about some the difficult choices he had made in his time as a soldier. He gave this important piece of wisdom and advice.

"I have been following your career as a soldier, let's compare. I was an overgrown boy hardly 16 when I first put on a uniform. Rode all night after entraining guns, horses and equipment riding freight to Sussex. First food at 6 PM next day. Beans baked by Dan Gallagher may have been a bit sour in the July heat. Sick, and so homesick. I never missed a camp. Last camp 1914. I had contracted typhoid with pneumonia, so did not get in the army until 1916. Got back to Halifax in 1919 on May 24th, 28 years old."

"During that time I had never got interested in any girl enough to go head over heals. We will say I danced with a good many, kissed a few. One, we even talked about how many kids we would like to have, but we never even kissed."

(Your Grandmother) "Myrtle and I met and were congenial. Wrote over 100 letters during the war. When I returned, met the other one. She had waited. We went to each other's arms, but the thrill was not there. But Myrtle and I grew together. I was older. Three years away had aged me more than she had at her age. It was rugged at times but hard and family kept us from failing."

Myrtle Olmstead and Walter Estabrooks, 1919.

"How can I advise you. The army will become less thrilling all the time. There is nothing that can compare with the satisfaction of making a home. There are heights one can reach in business, but nothing compares with the joy of love and home with a partner not too much younger. We have met Faye and could love her like one of our own family. Look ahead to making life enjoyable for her and you will be surprised at the kick you will get out of it yourself. Hope this catches up with you. Get a permanent address and start living. Gramp."

Order of Battle of the Canadian Army during World War One

Order of Battle, Canadian Army Corps, 1914-1918
Corps Headquarters
General Officer Commanding: Lieutenant-General Sir A.W. Currie:
Brigadier-General, General Staff: Brigadier-General P.P. deB. Radcliffe;
Deputy Adjutant and Quartermaster-General: Brigadier-General G.J. Farmer;
General Officer Commanding Royal Artillery: Brigadier-General E.W.B. Morrison;
Chief Engineer: Brigadier-General W.B. Lindsay

Corps Troops
CAVALRY
Royal Canadian Dragoons
Lord Strathcona's Horse
Fort Garry Horse
Canadian Light Horse
Royal North-West Mounted Police Squadron

ARTILLERY
Royal Canadian Horse Artillery Brigade
8th Army Brigade, Canadian Field Artillery (CFA)
    24th, 30th, **32nd Field Batteries** (W.R. Estabrooks unit)
    42nd Howitzer Battery
"E" Anti-Aircraft Battery

Corps Heavy Artillery
1st Brigade, Canadian Garrison Artillery (CGA)
   1st, 3rd, 7th, 9th Siege Batteries
2nd Brigade, CGA
   1st, 2nd Heavy Batteries
   2nd, 4th, 5th, 6th Siege Batteries
3rd Brigade, CGA
   8th, 10th, 11th, 12th Siege Batteries

Fifth Divisional Artillery
13th Brigade, CFA
   52nd, 53rd, 55th Field Batteries
   51st Howitzer Battery
14th Brigade, CFA
   60th, 61st, 66th Field Batteries
   58th Howitzer Battery

ENGINEERS

MACHINE-GUN CORPS
1st Canadian Motor Machine-Gun Brigade
   "A", "B", Borden, Eaton, Yukon Batteries
1st, 2nd, 3rd, 4th, 5th, 6th, 7th, 8th, 9th, 10th, 11th, 12th, 13th, 14th, 15th, 16th Machine-Gun Companies
ARMY SERVICE CORPS

MEDICAL CORPS
Numbers 1,2,3,6,7,8 General Hospitals
Numbers 2,3,7,8,9,10 Stationary Hospitals
Numbers 1,2,3,4 Casualty Clearing Stations
7th (Cavalry) Field Ambulance
14th Field Ambulance

Divisional Troops

FIRST CANADIAN DIVISION: Major-General A.C. Macdonell
First Infantry Brigade (Brigadier-General W.A. Griesbach)
    1st (Western Ontario) Battalion
    2nd (Eastern Ontario) Battalion
    3rd (Toronto Regiment) Battalion
    4th (Central Ontario) Battalion
    1st Trench Mortar Battery
Second Infantry Brigade (Brigadier-General F.O.W. Loomis)
    5th (Western Cavalry) Battalion
    7th (1st British Columbia Regiment) Battalion
    8th (90th Winnipeg Rifles) Battalion
    10th (Canadians) Battalion
    2nd Trench Mortar Battery
Third Infantry Brigade (Brigadier-General G.S. Tuxford)
    13th (Royal Highlanders of Canada) Battalion
    14th (Royal Montreal Regiment) Battalion
    15th (48th Highlanders of Canada) Battalion
    16th (Canadian Scottish) Battalion
    3rd Trench Mortar Battery
1st Brigade, CFA
    1st, 3rd, 4th Field Batteries
    2nd Howitzer Battery
2nd Brigade, CFA
    5th, 6th, 7th Field Batteries
    48th Howitzer Battery
1st, 2nd, 3rd Field Ambulances

SECOND CANADIAN DIVISION: Major-General H.E. Burstall
Fourth Infantry Brigade (Brigadier-General R. Rennie)
    18th (Western Ontario) Battalion

19th (Central Ontario) Battalion
20th (Central Ontario) Battalion
21st (Eastern Ontario) Battalion
4th Trench Mortar Battery
Fifth Infantry Brigade (Brigadier-General J.M. Ross)
22nd (French Canadian) Battalion
24th (Victoria Rifles of Canada) Battalion
25th (Nova Scotia Rifles) Battalion
26th (New Brunswick) Battalion
5th trench Mortar Battery
Sixth Infantry Brigade (Brigadier-General H.D.B. Ketchen)
27th (Winnipeg) Battalion
28th (Northwest) Battalion
29th (Vancouver) Battalion
31st (Alberta) Battalion
6th Trench Mortar Battery
5th Brigade, CFA
17th, 18th, 20th Field Batteries
23rd Howitzer Battery
6th Brigade, CFA
15th, 16th, 25th Field Batteries
22nd Howitzer Battery
4th, 5th, 6th Field Ambulances

THIRD CANADIAN DIVISION: Major-General L.J. Lipsett
Seventh Infantry Brigade (Brigadier-General H.M. Dyer)
Royal Canadian Regiment
Princess Patricia's Canadian Light Infantry
42nd (Royal Highlanders of Canada) Battalion
49th (Edmonton Regiment) Battalion
7th Trench Mortar Battery
Eighth Infantry Brigade (Brigadier-General J.H. Elmsley)

1st Canadian Mounted Rifles
2nd Canadian Mounted Rifles
4th Canadian Mounted Rifles
8th Canadian Mounted Rifles
Ninth Infantry Brigade (Brigadier-General F.W. Hill)
    43rd (Cameron Highlanders of Canada) Battalion
    52nd (Ontario) Battalion
    58th (Central Ontario) Battalion
    116th (Ontario) Battalion
    9th Trench Mortar Battery
9th Brigade, CFA
    31st, 33rd, 45th Field Batteries
    36th Howitzer Battery
10th Brigade, CFA
    38th, 39th, 40th Field Batteries
    35th Howitzer battery
8th, 9th, 10th Field Ambulances

FOURTH CANADIAN DIVISION: Major-General D. Watson
Tenth Infantry Brigade (Brigadier-General E. Hilliam)
    44th (Manitoba) Battalion
    46th (South Saskatchewan) Battalion
    47th (British Columbia) Battalion
    50th (Calgary) Battalion
    10th Trench Mortar Battery
Eleventh Infantry Brigade (Brigadier-General V.W. Odlum)
    54th (Central Ontario) Battalion
    75th (Mississauga) Battalion
    87th (Canadian Grenadier Guards) Battalion
    102nd (Central Ontario) Battalion
    11th Trench Mortar Battery
Twelfth Infantry Brigade (Brigadier-General J.H. MacBrien)

38th (Ottawa) Battalion
72nd (Seaforth Highlanders of Canada) Battalion
78th (Winnipeg Grenadiers) Battalion
85th (Nova Scotia Highlanders) Battalion
12th Trench Mortar Battery
3rd Brigade, CFA
   10th, 11th, 12th Field Batteries
   9th Howitzer Battery
4th Brigade, CFA
   13th, 19th, 27th Field Batteries
   21st Howitzer Battery
11th, 12th, 13th Field Ambulances

Background to the Estabrooks family name

Walter traces his ancestry back beyond Elijah and the Estabrooks family that settled on the Saint John River in 1763. The name originated in Flanders, where Estauberg (d') or Estaubrugge was the name of one of the confederate nobles. He apparently belonged to the family or clan d'Estambrugge, to which Oliver d'Estambrugge, who was appointed bailiff of Ghent in 1387, belonged. Heer van Estambrugge may have been a brother of the Count Van Ligne, in which case he later broke away from the confederates, as in the latter part of 1566, he assumed command of 100 Cavalry from the National Militia, for the defence of Brussels.[162]

In the Middle Ages, several Flemish families by the name of Yandell (or Yendall) lived together long ago in the low countries of Europe (Holland or Flanders) in the neighbourhood of Ghent or Liege. They were Dutch-Flemings. The main body of the family lived on the west side of a stream; but a considerable number lived on the east side at the end of a particular bridge (or bridges), and were therefore called the Estenbrugge-Yandells or briefly, the Estenbrugge.

At the time of the Reformation, (about 1517), these people became Protestants. During the religious wars that followed (about 1570-80), and the activity of the Spanish Inquisition during the latter half of the sixteenth century, they had to leave the country. A large group went together and settled in western Devon. Some used the name Yandell and some the name Estenbrugge, which gradually became Anglicized into various forms of Estabrooks.

The tradition Florence Estabrooks received was that the Estenbrugge or Yandells lived in Brugges, Liege or Ghent (in present day Belgium). Another tradition however, is that they originally lived in Holland, moved into Flanders, and after a brief stay went on to England. Both branches of the family had members who migrated to America, where they apparently kept some contact.

Estabrooks in North America

Joseph Estabrook of Concord, Massachusetts was born at Enfield, Middlesex County, England in 1640. His father was also probably born in England, but his grandfather may have been born in Flanders, placing the original emigration some time between 1590 and 1600. The family must have done well in England, as Joseph was prepared for college before coming to America and took his four-year course after his arrival. His brother Thomas also did well, as he bought a large farm near Concord.

Joseph's parents were certainly Puritans. After the death of Cromwell and the Restoration of Charles II, it was the sensible thing for a person wishing to be a clergyman in the Congregationalist Church to come to Boston, Massachusetts.

Joseph arrived in Boston in 1660, and attended Harvard College from which he graduated in 1664. In 1667 he was ordained as a colleague of the Reverend Peter Bulkeley at Concord, and on Bulkeley's death in 1696 became pastor of the Church, continuing in that office until his death 16 September 1711 at the age of 71 years. He had been made a freeman at Cambridge, Mass on 03 May 1665. On 20 May 1668, he married Mary Mason, daughter of Captain Hugh and Esther Mason, at Watertown, Mass.

The "Boston News" reported that the Reverend Joseph Estabrook "was eminent for his skill in the Hebrew language, a most orthodox, learned, and worthy divine; of excellent principles in religion, indefatigably laborious in the ministry of holy life and conversation."

Children of Joseph and Mary: Joseph; Benjamin (who attended Harvard in 1690, then became a minister at Lexington, and died in 1697); Mary; Samuel (who also attended Harvard in 1696, and became a minister at Canterbury, Connecticut from 1711 to 1727); Daniel; and Ann.

Joseph (junior) was born in Concord, Massachusetts on 06 May 1669. He married his first wife, Milicent Woods on 31 December 1689, at Cambridge Farms, Massachusetts and they had six children. Milicent was the daughter of Henry W. Woods of Connecticut, and she died at Concord on 26 March 1692. Joseph later married Hannah Leavitt, daughter of John Leavitt of Hingham. Hannah was the widow of Joseph Loring and had a daughter by her first husband named Submit. Submit later married Joseph's son by Milicent Woods, Joseph junior.

Joseph bought a farm of two hundred acres of land in Lexington in 1693. The Concord Road bound it on the southwest. He was an active and influential member of the Church at Lexington and represented it on many public occasions. He commanded a military company, and filled the office of town clerk, treasurer, assessor, selectman and representative to the General Court. He was a man of more than ordinary education and was engaged to teach the first man's school in the town. He died in Lexington on 23 September 1733.

Children of **Joseph** and **Milicent**: Joseph (the third); John; Solomon; Hannah (who married Joseph Frost of Sherburne); Milicent; and **Elijah**.

Elijah, son of Joseph (the second) and Hannah (Leavitt) Loring, was born in Lexington on 25 August 1703. He married Hannah Daniel of Sherburne (born 06 April 1702), in Boston on 01 October 1724. Their place of residence is unknown between 1724 and 1734, and there is a tradition that after their marriage, Elijah and his wife went to England, where their son Elijah (junior) was born. It is said that they returned to America in 1730.

While in England Elijah probably visited Flemish relatives, for his son Elijah (junior) was very well versed in Flemish traditions, which he told to his grandchildren. The American tradition is that the Elijah Estabrooks who came to the Saint John River was pro-British.

A short time after his return, Elijah (senior) was with his wife's people, the Daniels, and his brother-in-law, Joseph Frost in Sherburne. His daughter Hannah was born in Sherburne in 1734. Not long afterwards, Elijah (senior) died 01 December 1740 in Sherburne.

An entry in the Newbury, Massachusetts records states that Joseph Burril of Haverhill married Mrs. Hannah Esterbrook in Newbury on 09 February 1743/44. They lived in East Haverhill (Rocks Village). This Hannah may have been the widow of Elijah (senior); hence Elijah (junior), Submit and Samuel turn up in Haverhill.

Elijah senior's journeys must have depleted his resources, as he died intestate and his estate was small. It was administered by Joseph Frost.

Children of Elijah and Hannah: Mary; **Elijah**; Deborah; Submit; Hannah; Joseph; Samuel; and Aaron.

In the Middlesex County Probate Records (1st series), v.24, p. 157 (Cambridge, Mass), the following entry appears:

Middlesex

S.S. Guardianship to Elijah (at his own election) a minor in his 19th year of age, son of Elijah Estherbrook (sic) late of Sherburne in said County Dec'd., Is committed to Joseph Frost of Sherburne aforesaid.

Gent. who hath given bond of 500 (pounds).

Witness my hand and seal of office

Dated at Cambr. the 14th July 1746.

S. Danforth J. Probt.

Born about 1727, as a boy before the death of his father, **Elijah** (junior) must have been in Sherburne with his family between 1734 and 1740. During this time he acquired a good education for his journal is well written. After his father's death, his uncle Joseph Frost or the Daniels probably looked after him. The formal guardianship assumed in 1746 was "probably a surety for him going out into the world."[163]

Elijah soon found his way to Haverhill. His mother was there and there was plenty of work in connection with shipbuilding. He was admitted to the Second Church (Congregational) at East Salisbury on 04 March 1750. He married **Mary** Hackett of Salisbury on 14 November 1750, with the wedding ceremony being performed at Haverhill, Massachusetts, although it is recorded in the Second Church at Salisbury.

The family apparently lived in East Haverhill from 1750 to about 1757 as the baptisms of the first three children are recorded in the Fourth Church (Congregational): Hannah, baptized 25 August 1751; Molly, baptized 18 March 1753, and Elijah, baptized 23 May 1756. Elijah then appears to have moved to Boxford, close to Bradford, about 1727, as baptisms of two of his children appear in the records of the Second Church (Congregational) in Boxford: Samuel, baptized 11 December 1757, and **Ebenezer**, baptized 09 September 1759.

Elijah's wife, Mary Hackett, was born in Salisbury 01 August 1728. She was the daughter of Ebenezer and Hannah (Ring) Hackett, and her family were ship-builders.

Elijah's diary records two periods of service; he completed his first tour of duty (after the battle at Ticonderoga) on 07 November 1758 and re-enlisted 06 April 1759. He went by ship to Halifax and during his tour of duty in Nova Scotia he became a Sergeant. His family remained in Boxford. He left Nova Scotia 25 November 1760 and arrived home 15 December.

During the next two and a half years, Elijah made preparations to move his family the Saint John River, an area that was still called Nova Scotia. Governor Lawrence of Nova Scotia was urged by the Lords of Trade and Plantations to re-people the lands vacated by the French with settlers from New England. Colonel McNutt went through the Essex County section of Massachusetts urging men to better their fortunes. In the Newbury-Haverhill district, a group organized and decided to examine the situation. In the winter of 1761-1762, the Governor of Massachusetts appointed Israel Perley in charge of 12 men in the pay of

Massachusetts to make a snowshoe journey through the wilderness from Maine to the Saint John River. Hugh Quinton was one of this party.[164]

Elijah was also one of this group. They went by boat to Machias and made their way by trails until they descended the Oromocto River. The Township of Maugerville, twelve miles long and twelve miles wide was laid out in lots early in 1762. On Wednesday, 06 October 1762, the signers of the agreement met at the house of Daniel Ingalls, inn-holder in Andover, at 10 AM to draw their lots.[165]

Early in 1763 Elijah moved his family to Halifax and then to Cornwallis, intending to leave them there until he had prepared for them in Maugerville Township. He crossed the bay and joined Israel Perley's party, which was going up the river to occupy the land. It is said that he took his son, Elijah, a boy of seven or eight years, with him to see the country.

When they reached the township Elijah found that his lot near Jemseg was under water. This must have been a great disappointment. He decided not to use the lot and returned to Cornwallis.

During the next two years Elijah was apparently exploring the possibilities of the new land. Tradition says that he paid a visit to Sackville, where Valentine Estabrooks had settled. His heart however, was apparently set on the river. On 18 October 1765, Elijah went to work in the store of Simonds and White at Portland Point. In 1789 he participated in a meeting concerning local improvements, as a member of the Portland Board of Trade executive committee and consulting member.[166]

In the summer of 1769 the Reverend Thomas Wood, a clergyman of the Church of England, visited the Saint John River. At Portland Point he held a Sunday service on 02 July, and baptized John and Abigail, children of Elijah and Mary Estabrooks. Sarah may also have been baptized at that time.

In 1773 Elijah made an agreement with Wm. Hazen and James Simonds to settle in the Township of Conway near the mouth of the river, Hazen and Simonds guaranteeing him a deed of 250 acres of land. An old return or census dated 01 August 1775 shows that he had cleared and improved seven acres of land and built a log house.

The lot granted to Elijah was No. 5, next to the shipbuilding plant and possibly included the modern Saint John Market Square. The lot next to him, No. 6, was granted to his son-in-law, Zebedee Ring.

Hazen and Simonds ran an extensive business as a fur trading company and fishery, and they were anxious to place settlers on the land because it was in danger of being escheated.

The American Revolution began to have an impact on the Saint John River in the month of August 1775, when a raiding party from Machias, Maine, entered the harbour in a sloop and burned Fort Frederick on the Conway side. The raiders also captured a brig in the harbour loaded with provisions for the British troops in Boston. The inhabitants of Conway took to the woods avoid the depredations of the marauders.

This was the first act of aggression in the Bay of Fundy, and it produced a great sensation; but the experience was repeated many times and must have been painfully reminiscent of the Indian raids on Haverhill in the early years of its existence. The privateers were just as rapacious as the Indians in their looting, in spite of the fact that many of the river people sympathized with the American cause.

In 1776 an expedition was sent against the English at Fort Cumberland on the Chignecto Isthmus where Lieutenant Colonel Goreham was in command, but it was beaten off and it returned to the river. Major Studholme's report shows that Elijah Estabrooks (junior) was one of those who accompanied Hugh Quinton on this expedition.

In May 1777, John Allan, one of the most determined of the American sympathizers, set out from Machias with 43 men in four whaleboats and several canoes. They arrived at Musquash Cove on 01 June, crossed the river at Indiantown, and then made their way to Portland Point where they took Hazen, Simonds and White prisoners. They spent some time on the river before leaving. After this experience

Simonds moved up the river to Sheffield where he bought a section of land between the Maugerville Township and Loder Creek from the Morris grant. He built a log cabin on the bank of the river and lived there for nine years. Elijah left Conway at the same time, and settled on land which was part of the Spry grant at Gagetown on Grimross Neck.

Elijah's family was growing up and leaving home. Hannah married Zebedee Ring in Salisbury in 1772. They settled next to her father in Conway and in 1777 moved to Sheffield. Mary married Samuel Hart of Maugerville in 1773. Elijah (junior) married Mary Whittemore in 1777 and after a brief period in Jemseg settled just below James Simonds on the river. **Ebenezer** married Maria Fletcher in 1782 and settled near his father on Gagetown Neck. Still at home were Joseph (age 15), Sarah (age 13), Abigail (age 11), John (age 9), and Deborah (age 3).

The rugged life proved to be too much for Elijah's wife, Mary Hackett, and she died in 1778. She was probably buried in the Garrison graveyard as it was the oldest Protestant graveyard in this part of the country, and Elijah himself was later buried there. She had impressed her children as a woman of courage and resource, and "Mary Hackett" is a name found frequently among her descendants.

Archilaus Hammond, himself an ex-soldier, had settled in the Gagetown area before Elijah moved there. The Hammonds came from Marblehead. His sister Sarah was baptized there 21 October 1739. On 24 September 1764, she married James Oakes. They moved from Marblehead to Cornwallis and quite possibly encountered Elijah and Mary Estabrooks there. Sarah had four children by James Oakes: James (junior), Benjamin, Sarah and Christopher (Christopher was born in 1773). James (senior) died about the same time as Mary Hackett. Sarah Oakes brought her small family to Gagetown and married Elijah Estabrooks on 17 December 1778. They had a further two children, Elizabeth (Betsy) born 30 October 1779, and Hammond, born 29 January 1783.

In the year 1765, shortly after the close of the Seven Years War, enormous tracts of land, called Townships, were granted in the Saint John River valley to officers and government officials. The arrival of the Loyalists in 1783 led to most of these grants being escheated excepting where settlers were in actual possession.

Governor Parr decreed that such lots as were occupied by old inhabitants of the country should not be appropriated by Loyalists without paying for improvements. A commission was appointed to assess values:

Report of the Commission to Investigate Pre-Loyalist Settlements:

For Gagetown, 30 June 1783:

Elijah Easterbrook (sic) has a wife and eight children, a log house with two rooms and about twelve acres of land cleared. Came from Cornwallis about 16 years past; settled at the mouth of the river and says he was drove up by rebels.

For the Township of Conway, 08 July 1783:

Elijah Easterbrook settled in consequence of an agreement with Hazen and Simonds. Cleared and improved about seven acres of land and built a log house which is now fallen to decay, said Easterbrook moving up the river on account of the danger of his situation. Had lived on it eight years.

Governor Carleton and his Council continued the policy of Governor Parr after the formation of the Province of New Brunswick. Elijah Estabrooks' house was valued at 10 pounds and his improvements at 48 pounds. Walter Chase, the Loyalist on whose grant his land was situated, was unwilling to pay this amount and Elijah was confirmed in possession of his land in 1784. This was Lot No. 5, Grimross Neck. The Loyalists however, were determined to get rid of pre-Loyalists and Elijah found things very unpleasant.

Actual riots took place and some belligerents were put in jail. Elijah applied for a new allotment. He received some compensation in Cambridge, which included one-half of lots 25 and 26. His sons

Ebenezer (25) and Joseph (26) received the other halves. Elijah junior was granted one-half of lot 3 at Jemseg, Parish of Waterborough and lot 32 on the interval.

Archelaus Hammond moved to Kingsclear at the same time. He received one lot there and his eldest son received another.

The lots in Cambridge were beautifully situated on a ridge overlooking the Jemseg river at its entrance to Grand Lake. The Garrison graveyard was just over the fence on a slope stretching down to a creek.

Elijah moved with his family and two married sons, Ebenezer and Joseph, to these lots in 1787. Elijah apparently left the management of his lots mainly to his Oakes stepsons and his wife. He himself spent much of his time with his eldest son Elijah Junior, and John his youngest son by Mary Hackett in Canning.

John was seeking to establish himself. He had no love for the water-soaked interval and early in his married life moved across the river to land just above Swan Creek. He built the first frame house in that part of the country.

Elijah Estabrooks thus spent his old age close to all his children. His younger daughters were married; Sarah married John Marsh on 15 July 1790 and lived in Canning; Abigail married Wm. Harper in Canning in 1794; Deborah married Moses Clarke junior in August 1796; Elizabeth married Martin Olts, junior on 29 March 1796. They lived at French Lake and then on Nashwaak.

Elijah remained hale and hearty to the last. Mrs. Abraham Estabrooks, who married his grandson, said that he used to tell tales of old times to his grandchildren. She said there were two things that he used to pray for: one was that he should never be sick and the other was that he should die at his work. He used to pound up grain for chickens in a mortar. One afternoon after working for awhile, he lay back in his chair and covered his face with his hat. His grandchildren, who were playing around, thought that he was asleep; but when they went to wake him for supper, they found that he was dead. He was buried in the garrison graveyard at Jemseg.

Elijah died intestate. By a deed dated 11 August 1796 and signed by all his sons and daughters with their wives and husbands his estate was given to his widow, Sarah. This deed was probably drawn up on the day of his funeral.

His chief assets were the two half lots in Cambridge. His widow sold these to her sons James and Benjamin Oakes in 1803. James had married Rachel Olts 07 July 1792. The Oakes men probably lived there until 1813 when they sold the lots to Archelaus Purdy and moved up to Carleton County. The Estabrooks men sold theirs about the same time, and moved up to Wakefield, Carleton County. Some of the Oakes men went on to Ontario.

Sarah (Oakes) Estabrooks may also be buried in the Garrison graveyard.

Florence Estabrooks tried to locate the site of Elijah's burial. Fragments of a gravestone with Elijah Estabrooks name had been scattered in the graveyard located on Jefferson Dykeman's farm. The graves were clearly defined but the stones were gone. Elijah's grave was about ten feet straight in front of the entrance. The tombstone had a curved top and the name clearly cut. Florence indicated that the place had grown up in 1951. As of the spring of the year 2000, an old oak tree still stands guard over the gravesites of Elijah and possibly both of his wives. The site is located just across the bridge at Jemseg, and is marked as the "Old Garrison Cemetery," although none of the original stones are still standing.

Elijah's children:
(By Mary Hackett): Hannah, Mary, Sarah, Elijah, Samuel, **Ebenezer**, Joseph, and Sarah, Abigail, John, Deborah; (by Sarah Hammond-Oakes): Elizabeth, and Hammond.

Elijah's son Ebenezer was baptized in Boxford, Massachusetts, 28 August 1759. He married Maria Fletcher before 1783 and they had nine children. They settled on Gagetown Neck, but were dispossessed by the Loyalists in 1785. He settled for a time on his grant in Cambridge (half of Lot 25); but by 1796 he was living in Lakeville, Sheffield. He was one of those who signed the covenant of the Church at Waterborough 20 October 1800. This was the occasion of forming the Baptist Church. He moved to Lincoln about 1808. In the same year he received land on Little River. On 25 December 1813 Ebenezer Estabrooks and a number of others applied to be dismissed from the church at Canning to join in forming a Baptist Church in Fredericton. This was the beginning of the Brunswick St. Baptist Church. In 1816, Ebenezer took up a large farm in Jacksontown, Parish of Wakefield, Carleton County, where he died about 1851. About 1814 he married a second time; his second wife was Charlotte Ann Lounsbury, born 1782, died 1860. Ebenezer and Charlotte Ann had another five children. After Ebenezer's death, Charlotte Ann lived with the Rideouts, dying about 1860 at the age of 90.

Ebenezer's children:
(By Maria Fletcher): Ebenezer, Maria, David E., Thomas Fletcher, Stephen Potter, Joseph Fletcher, William Wilmot, Deborah, and Harriet; (by Charlotte Ann Lounsbury): Ebenezer, **Chipman**, Sarah, George, and Charlotte Ann.

Chipman was born 16 December 1818. He married Lucretia Smith 01 May 1849 in Houlton, Maine, and lived in Waterville, Carleton County, where they had 12 children. Chipman died in Waterville 13 December 1890.

Chipman's children:
(By Lucretia Smith): Albert, Ebenezer, Stephen, Frederick, Wilson, John, Clara, Amelia, **Joseph**, Sophia, Annie, and Rhoda.

Joseph was born 18 September 1861 and married **Catherine** Peed. They had three children. Joseph and his sister Sophia were twins. Joseph died 12 January 1939, Catherine died in 1950.

Background to the Estabrooks family name 113

Joseph and Catherine's children:
Walter, Minnie, and Frank.
Walter married **Myrtle** Olmstead
Walter and Myrtle's children:
Kathyrn, Gaynelle, Frederick, **Beatrice**, Bernard and Wilhelmine.
Beatrice Leah Estabrook married **Aage** C. Skaarup
Beatrice and Aage's children:
Harold, Dale and Christopher.
Harold[167] married **Faye** Jenkins
Harold and Faye's children:
Jonathan and Sean

Jonathan and Sean photographed in 1990 at Vimy Ridge where their great-grandfather Walter Estabrooks fought during the Great War.

Epilogue

Postscript

Walter Estabrooks was not the first of his line to keep a diary and to see battle. On 07 July 1758, his great grandfather **Elijah Estabrooks** fought Montcalm at Ticonderoga. Although his Company of Massachusetts Provincials gave a good account of themselves, the British force lost that particular battle. Elijah went on to serve in Halifax during the war that won Canada from France for Britain. His diary is also available in a similar format. The following is an extract from Elijah's journal:

07 July 1758

...And the 7th day we marched off to Ticonderoga,—and we marched about 4 miles up to the mills—and there built a bridge and a breast work—and I went with a small party of about 25 of our men in order to make what discovery we could of the French at their advance guard—and three of the party crept up so near that they fired at 8 who were sitting on a log and judged that they killed seven of them—for they perceived but one to rise and go away, which caused us to retreat as fast as we could—the French and Indians following us with hideous noise—about a-mile-and-a-half—and after our return we had orders from Colonel Broadstreet for our Provincials to march off for the fort—and it was reported the French had deserted their fort and were gone away in their bateaux for Crown Point and we also marched off about one mile to the top of a hill—about one mile from the French advance guard—and built a breast-work and camped there that night—and the 8th day we marched from there up the road within a quarter of a mile of the French advance guard, and drew up a line from Lake

Champlain to the great Lake Haricon all our Provincials and Colonel Purdy's and Major Roger's Rangers were drawn up in a line about 30 rods within us—and they crept up and shot down several of their sentries—and we had orders to keep our lines—and not to advance—nor fire a gun on pain of death—until the regulars with the Rangers had gone up and set the battle in array—and if they were too strong for them they were to retreat in our rear—and then we were to advance in order to drive them back until they had recruited (regrouped?)—but when the general came up with the regulars, he ordered the whole of our Provincials on the right wing—and the regulars with the Rangers on the left wing—and we marched within 30 or 40 rods of the French trenches and set the battle in array—and we had about as smart a fight for about 4 hours as ever was heard or seen in England, Flanders or America—and the French prevailed very much—but it was through deceit—for they acted contrary to the acts of all kings and parliaments—for in the midst of their fight they hoisted an English flag in their trench only to deceive us, and so it did, for we thought that they had given up—and drew up and was going to take possession—when all at once they hauled that down and hoisted their own, and with a great hellish shout poured a volley upon us, and killed more at that time than they had before—2541 of our men they killed and wounded 1473, but through the goodness of God we had not one killed nor wounded in our company.[168]

...In Walter Estabrooks own words, "that's all!"
Harold A. Skaarup, 27 March 2000

Afterword

One of the things about listening and learning is that the older one grows, the more you should listen to those who don't talk much. Quite often they have learned things the hard way that we can all benefit from. Many of Walter's companions did not come back, and those that did all had stories to tell. I think the story that he told me about carrying the corrugated metal on his first trip up to the front lines struck closest to home. In his diary entry for 13 January 1917, he spoke of how there was a loud "POP!" up front, and all the experienced hands around him suddenly froze. Not realizing the ominous consequences of the sound, being a "new guy" (and we have all been there), he kept plodding along and ran into the man frozen like a statue in front of him. Of course the crash of the metal and the banging sounds drew a terrible response. Everyone had stopped as the flare lit the sky. Someone asked, "What fool did not know enough to stop when he heard a flare pistol?" A machine-gun then sprayed all of them with deadly fire for about a minute. No one answered the question, but as Walter pointed out, "he had learned his first lesson." Sometimes one is permitted a mistake or two. The trick to surviving is in doing one's best not to repeat them. Grant that neither our children nor we have to learn from these same kinds of mistakes, but in the process, do our best to ensure that "this day, nobody dies."
Hal Skaarup

About the Author

Major Hal Skaarup

If you would like to know a bit about the author's background, the following is a brief summary. For those of you who prefer a longer biography, I regret that the following history does not mention any of the many and much more interesting people I have known or met. I am sure they could tell a better story.

Major Hal Skaarup is an Army officer presently serving in the Intelligence Branch of the Canadian Forces (CF). His interest in storytelling comes from his parents, Aage and Beatrice Skaarup, musicians and storytellers extraordinary. His father, Warrant Officer Aage Skaarup (now retired) served in the Royal Canadian Air Force (RCAF) and this meant that he, his mother and two brothers, moved a lot. Born in Woodstock, New Brunswick, he went to school in various locations. He attended Widdifield High School in North Bay, Ontario and Moosehorn Collegiate Institute while living at Canadian Forces Station (CFS) Gypsumville, Manitoba.

Hal joined the Reserve Army (Militia) while attending The College of Trades and Technology (CT&T) in St. John's, Newfoundland in 1971. He later became an army officer through the Reserve Officer University Training Program (ROUTP) in Halifax, and after completing his basic officer training at Shilo, Manitoba, was commissioned into the Canadian Forces (CF) in 1973. In 1974 he completed his Bachelor of Fine Arts (BFA) degree, graduating from the Nova Scotia College of Art and Design (NSCAD) in Halifax, Nova Scotia. Between 1977 and 1981 he was a member of the Canadian Forces Parachute Team (CFPT), the "Skyhawks," participating in airshows across Canada and parts of

United States. He is still an active skydiver with more than 1600 jumps to date.

Hal transferred to the Regular Army following a two year tour of duty with the Canadian Forces in Europe (CFE), in Lahr, Germany in 1983. From there he was sent to the Canadian Forces School of Intelligence and Security (CFSIS), first as a student, and later as an instructor. Between 1984 and 1986 he served as an intelligence analyst in Ottawa and then from 1986 to 1989 as the Regimental Intelligence Officer (R Int O) for the Canadian Airborne Regiment (CAR). As a Captain in the CAR, Hal went to the island of Cyprus on United Nation's (UN) duty for six months from August 1986 to February 87. In 1998, all UN Peacekeepers including Hal and his comrades were awarded the Nobel Peace Prize. That same year he completed the Canadian Forces Staff School (CFSS) course in Toronto. One year later he also completed the six months Canadian Land Forces Command and Staff Course in Kingston (CLFCSC) which is also known to Army Officers as "Fox Hole U."

On completing CLFCSC in 1989 Hal returned to Lahr, Germany as the Intelligence officer for 4 Canadian Mechanized Brigade Group (4 CMBG) with the First Canadian Division (1 Cdn Div) Forward. This came at one of the most interesting periods of change in modern European history. The Berlin Wall came down, Russia's President Gorbachev resigned, and the Gulf War came and went. In 1992, he was posted back to CFSIS. On promotion to Major in 1993, he became the Officer Commanding (OC) the Intelligence Training Company, and later the Distance Learning Company. In 1994, Major Skaarup was posted to CFB Gagetown, as the Intelligence Directing Staff (Int DS) officer in the Tactics School at the Combat Training Centre (CTC), dual-hatted as the Base G2. Between instructing on and participating in numerous field exercises as the commander of the "Enemy Forces," he completed his Master of Arts Degree (MA) in War Studies through the Royal Military College (RMC), graduating in May 1997. Between June and December 1997 he was posted to Sarajevo on a six month tour of duty as the Commanding Officer (CO) of the Canadian National Intelligence Centre (CANIC) in support of the Canadian Contingent of the NATO led Peace Stabilization Force (CC SFOR) in Bosnia-Herzegovina. This was perhaps the most interesting, challenging and in many ways rewarding of all the jobs and experiences he has had to date (and there are certainly more to come).

In June 1999, Major Skaarup completed the year long Land Forces Technical Staff Course (LFTSC) with RMC's Department of Applied Military Science (AMS) in Kingston. He is presently posted to Colorado where he is the Chief of the NORAD Exercise Intelligence Section, J2SZ on Cheyenne Mountain in Colorado Springs. Major Skaarup is a fledgling writer, and hopes to expand his skills in the story telling and writing business. If you are interested in more about his stories, his e-mail address is h.skaarup@worldnet.att.net.

Major Hal Skaarup and Sgt Chris Free, serving with the Canadian Contingent of the NATO-led Peace Stabilization Force (CC SFOR) in front of a destroyed BVP-80 East of Dubrovnik in Bosnia-Herzegovina, late fall 1997.

Bibliography

Goodspeed, LCol D.J. *The Armed Forces of Canada 1867-1967*, Directorate of History, Canadian Forces Headquarters, Ottawa, 1967.

Estabrooks, Walter R. *War Diary, 1916-1919*. Personal Notes and Papers.

Estabrooks, Florence C. *Estabrooks Family Vol 1*, 1952.

Notes

1. LCol D.J. Goodspeed, *The Armed Forces of Canada 1867-1967*, Directorate of History, Canadian Forces Headquarters, Ottawa, 1967, p. 29.
2. LCol D.J. Goodspeed, *The Armed Forces of Canada 1867-1967*, p. 29.
3. LCol D.J. Goodspeed, *The Armed Forces of Canada 1867-1967*, p. 29.
4. LCol D.J. Goodspeed, *The Armed Forces of Canada 1867-1967*, p. 67.
5. The Diary of Walter R. Estabrooks, 1916-1919. Personal Notes and Papers.
6. For information concerning the Flemish origin of the Estabrooks family name and Walter's ancestry, see Annex A.
7. For more on Elijah Estabrooks, a British-Massachusetts Provincial soldier who fought in the Seven Years War that led to the capture of Canada, see the *Journal of Elijah Estabrooks, 1758-59-60*.
8. For a list of the Canadian Army Order of Battle, see the Annex attached.
9. The site is now underwater in the St John River, due to the flooding from the Mactaquac dam near Fredericton.
10. Original book typed and bound by Wilhelmine Estabrooks, Walter Estabrooks youngest daughter.
11. LCol D.J. Goodspeed, The Armed Forces of Canada 1867-1967, Directorate of History, Canadian Forces Headquarters, Ottawa, 1967, p. 29.
12. Nitro-Cellu Tuluene.
13. Tri Nitro Tuluene.
14. Canadian Mounted Rifles, Royal Canadian Regiment and Princess Patricia's Canadian Light Infantry.
15. High explosive.

16. Haute-Avesnes is about 15 km West of Arras. Where possible, I have added the spelling of the present day city or place name in brackets along with, or instead of the original diary spelling. This is to aid the reader in finding the places mentioned in the diary on a current map. HAS.
17. This site is located a few kilometres North of Arras.
18. Observation Post
19. This site is located about 2 kilometres Northwest of Arras.
20. This site is located about 15 kilometres West of Arras & 2 kilometres below Auvigny-en-Artois.
21. Just North of Arras.
22. Brigade Headquarters.
23. This site is located about 10 kilometres West of Vimy near Neuville-St Vaast.
24. This site is located about 30 kilometres to the NorthWest.
25. This site is located about 8 kilometres Northwest of Arras.
26. This site is located about 15 kilometres Northwest of Arras.
27. This site is located about 2 kilometres Northwest of Liévin.
28. This site is located just below Bruay-en-Artois.
29. Liévin is the location of the site nick-named Whiz-Bang Corner.
30. 9th Brigade, Canadian Field Artillery, 45th Field Battery.
31. Just to the West of Bully-les-Mines.
32. Amettes is about 8 km Northwest of Auchel and about 2 km West of Ferfay.
33. Lillers is about 5 km North of Auchel.
34. This site is located about 8 kilometres due West of Liévin.
35. This site is located about 8 kilometres West of Vimy.
36. LCol D.J. Goodspeed, *The Armed Forces of Canada 1867-1967*, p. 43.
37. LCol D.J. Goodspeed, *The Armed Forces of Canada 1867-1967*, p. 43.
38. LCol D.J. Goodspeed, *The Armed Forces of Canada 1867-1967*, p 43-44.

39. Vimy Ridge is the site of the Canadian Army's greatest battle during World War One, in which all our Canadian overseas divisions participated. The ridge is situated about 8 kilometres South of Lens.
40. March 10th, 1917.
41. Just West of Souchez and South of Liévin.
42. This site is located about 8 kilometres West of Ablain-Saint-Nazaire.
43. This site is located about 4 kilometres West of Neuville-Saint-Vaast.
44. This site is located about 5 kilometres North of Arras.
45. 9th Brigade, CFA, under 3rd Division.
46. LCol D.J. Goodspeed, *The Armed Forces of Canada 1867-1967*, p. 44.
47. LCol D.J. Goodspeed, *The Armed Forces of Canada 1867-1967*, p. 44.
48. LCol D.J. Goodspeed, *The Armed Forces of Canada 1867-1967*, p. 44, 46.
49. LCol D.J. Goodspeed, *The Armed Forces of Canada 1867-1967*, p. 46.
50. LCol D.J. Goodspeed, *The Armed Forces of Canada 1867-1967*, p. 46.
51. LCol D.J. Goodspeed, *The Armed Forces of Canada 1867-1967*, p. 46.
52. LCol D.J. Goodspeed, *The Armed Forces of Canada 1867-1967*, p. 46.
53. LCol D.J. Goodspeed, *The Armed Forces of Canada 1867-1967*, p. 46.
54. LCol D.J. Goodspeed, *The Armed Forces of Canada 1867-1967*, p. 46.
55. LCol D.J. Goodspeed, *The Armed Forces of Canada 1867-1967*, p. 46, 48.
56. LCol D.J. Goodspeed, *The Armed Forces of Canada 1867-1967*, p. 48. Walter had his first good view of Vimy Ridge on 09 March, and tramped up on the "Pimple" on 10 March 1917. *W.R.E. Diary*, p. 8.
57. LCol D.J. Goodspeed, *The Armed Forces of Canada 1867-1967*, p. 48.
58. LCol D.J. Goodspeed, *The Armed Forces of Canada 1867-1967*, p. 49.
59. LCol D.J. Goodspeed, *The Armed Forces of Canada 1867-1967*, p. 49.
60. LCol D.J. Goodspeed, *The Armed Forces of Canada 1867-1967*, p. 49.
61. LCol D.J. Goodspeed, *The Armed Forces of Canada 1867-1967*, p. 49, 50.
62. LCol D.J. Goodspeed, *The Armed Forces of Canada 1867-1967*, p. 50.
63. LCol D.J. Goodspeed, *The Armed Forces of Canada 1867-1967*, p. 50.
64. LCol D.J. Goodspeed, *The Armed Forces of Canada 1867-1967*, p. 50.
65. This site is located about 10 kilometres West of Poperinge.
66. LCol D.J. Goodspeed, *The Armed Forces of Canada 1867-1967*, p. 50.

67. LCol D.J. Goodspeed, *The Armed Forces of Canada 1867-1967*, p. 50.
68. LCol D.J. Goodspeed, *The Armed Forces of Canada 1867-1967*, p. 51,52.
69. LCol D.J. Goodspeed, *The Armed Forces of Canada 1867-1967*, p. 52.
70. LCol D.J. Goodspeed, *The Armed Forces of Canada 1867-1967*, p. 52.
71. LCol D.J. Goodspeed, *The Armed Forces of Canada 1867-1967*, p. 52.
72. LCol D.J. Goodspeed, *The Armed Forces of Canada 1867-1967*, p. 53.
73. LCol D.J. Goodspeed, *The Armed Forces of Canada 1867-1967*, p. 53, 54.
74. LCol D.J. Goodspeed, *The Armed Forces of Canada 1867-1967*, p. 54.
75. LCol D.J. Goodspeed, *The Armed Forces of Canada 1867-1967*, p. 54.
76. LCol D.J. Goodspeed, *The Armed Forces of Canada 1867-1967*, p. 54.
77. LCol D.J. Goodspeed, *The Armed Forces of Canada 1867-1967*, p. 54.
78. LCol D.J. Goodspeed, *The Armed Forces of Canada 1867-1967*, p. 57.
79. On modern Belgian maps it is marked Passendale.
80. November 30th, 1917.
81. The German Army in World War One held 20 A7V heavy tanks, one A7V-U, and a few LK1s and LKII light tanks. Three German tank sections were assembled in 1917, six others (numbered eleven to 16) fought while using captured British Mk III and IV tanks (75 had been captured from the British by April 1918). The German tank units first went into action (using captured British Mark IV's) in France on 21 March 1918. On 24 April 1918, 13 A7V's went into battle in the Villers-Bretonneux sector. The Germans advanced steadily against the British Mk IVs and Whippets and accomplished the only German armoured success in World War One.
82. This site is located about 8 kilometres East of Hazebrouck.
83. This site is located about 5 kilometres Northwest of Bethune.
84. Major-General H.E. Burstall, Commander Second Canadian Division.
85. Harold was one of my father's three brothers (Frederick, Harold, Aage and Carl Skaarup). Harold served with the 8th Princess Louise (New Brunswick) Hussars, as a member of a Sherman tank crew in Italy. He and the members of his unit were shelled by German artillery during a battle in late August, 1944. Harold subsequently

died from the wounds he received on 06 September 1944, and he is presently buried in the Canadian War Cemetery in Monteccio, Italy. I was given his name as the first grandson in our family born after his death.
86. Frederick is my father's oldest brother, and in his late 80's is still an avid skier.
87. Kathryn is one Walter and Myrtle Estabrooks six children (Kathryn, Gaynelle, Frederick, Beatrice, Bernard and Wilhelmine).
88. Lieutenant-General Sir A.W. Currie was the General Officer Commanding the Canadian Army Corps.
89. This site is located about 8 kilometres Northwest of Vimy.
90. This site is located about 8 kilometres South of Auchel.
91. Brigadier-General E.W.B. Morrison, General Officer Commanding Royal Artillery.
92. 8th Army Brigade, Canadian Field Artillery.
93. Possibly 1st Canadian Motor Machine-Gun Brigade.
94. Walter was with the 32nd Battery.
95. Fifth Divisional Artillery, Canadian Army Corps.
96. Corps Heavy Artillery, possibly 1st, 2nd or 3rd Brigade, Canadian Garrison Artillery.
97. Possibly the 45th Field Battery, 9th Brigade.
98. Possibly the 46th (South Saskatchewan) Battalion from 4th Division.
99. Possibly the 49th (Edmonton Regiment) Battalion from 3rd Division.
100. Canada's Prime Minister, Sir Robert Borden.
101. Possibly the 29th (Vancouver) Battalion from 2nd Division.
102. This site is located about 15 kilometres Southwest of Arras.
103. This site is located about 10 kilometres Northwest of Arras.
104. LCol D.J. Goodspeed, *The Armed Forces of Canada 1867-1967*, p. 57, 58.
105. LCol D.J. Goodspeed, *The Armed Forces of Canada 1867-1967*, p. 58.
106. LCol D.J. Goodspeed, *The Armed Forces of Canada 1867-1967*, p. 58, 59.
107. Ludendorff later recalled that, "August 8th was the black day of the German Army." He confessed that the German war machine was

"no longer efficient" and that he could now see no successful outcome to the four-year old struggle. When the Kaiser was informed of this, he stated flatly: "The war must be ended." LCol D.J. Goodspeed, *The Armed Forces of Canada 1867-1967*, p. 59.
108. This road is now Highway 39.
109. This site is located about 15 kilometres Northwest of Arras.
110. This site is located about 20 kilometres East of Amiens.
111. This site is located midway between Amiens and Roye on highway 334.
112. LCol D.J. Goodspeed, *The Armed Forces of Canada 1867-1967*, p. 59.
113. LCol D.J. Goodspeed, *The Armed Forces of Canada 1867-1967*, p. 59, 61.
114. LCol D.J. Goodspeed, *The Armed Forces of Canada 1867-1967*, p. 61.
115. LCol D.J. Goodspeed, *The Armed Forces of Canada 1867-1967*, p. 61.
116. LCol D.J. Goodspeed, *The Armed Forces of Canada 1867-1967*, p. 61.
117. LCol D.J. Goodspeed, *The Armed Forces of Canada 1867-1967*, p. 61.
118. LCol D.J. Goodspeed, *The Armed Forces of Canada 1867-1967*, p. 61.
119. LCol D.J. Goodspeed, *The Armed Forces of Canada 1867-1967*, p. 61, 63.
120. LCol D.J. Goodspeed, *The Armed Forces of Canada 1867-1967*, p. 63.
121. LCol D.J. Goodspeed, *The Armed Forces of Canada 1867-1967*, p. 63.
122. LCol D.J. Goodspeed, *The Armed Forces of Canada 1867-1967*, p. 63.
123. LCol D.J. Goodspeed, *The Armed Forces of Canada 1867-1967*, p. 63.
124. LCol D.J. Goodspeed, *The Armed Forces of Canada 1867-1967*, p. 63.
125. Just Southwest of Roye.
126. This site is located just a few kilometres Northwest of Le Quesnel.
127. Just Northwest of Vrély.
128. This site is located 15 kilometres East of Amiens.
129. This site is located about 4 kilometres North of Villers-Bretonneux.
130. This site is located a few kilometres Southwest of Toutencourt.
131. This site is located about 10 kilometres East of Doullens.
132. This site is located about 15 kilometres West of Arras.
133. This site is on Highway 39, 10 kilometres East of Arras.

134. This site is located East of Arras and Monchy-le-Preux about 8 kilometres.
135. This site is located on the Southwest edge of the city of Arras.
136. This site is located a few kilometres South of Rémy.
137. This site is located South of Highway 39, 20 kilometres West of Arras.
138. This site is located South of Highway 39 and about 15 kilometres West of Cambrai.
139. This site is located on Highway 39 about 8 kilometres West of Cambrai.
140. Shellfire.
141. Diary entry for 02 October, 1918.
142. This site is located about 15 kilometres West of Arras, near Habarcq.
143. This site is located approximately 8 kilometres North of Cambrai.
144. Third Canadian Division, Eight Infantry Brigade, 1st, 2nd, 4th, 5th Canadian Mounted Rifles and 8th Trench Mortar Battery.
145. Major-General H.E. Burstall, Second Canadian Division.
146. This site is located about 10 kilometres Northwest of Cambrai.
147. Major-General L.J. Lipsett, Third Canadian Division.
148. LCol D.J. Goodspeed, *The Armed Forces of Canada 1867-1967*, p. 63.
149. LCol D.J. Goodspeed, *The Armed Forces of Canada 1867-1967*, p. 63.
150. LCol D.J. Goodspeed, *The Armed Forces of Canada 1867-1967*, p. 63, 64.
151. LCol D.J. Goodspeed, *The Armed Forces of Canada 1867-1967*, p. 64.
152. LCol D.J. Goodspeed, *The Armed Forces of Canada 1867-1967*, p. 64.
153. LCol D.J. Goodspeed, *The Armed Forces of Canada 1867-1967*, p. 64.
154. Burned up in a house fire, the remains of the 1916 model Erfurt Luger pistol were passed to Bernard Estabrooks, and then to Hal Skaarup, who restored it and had it registered. The pistol has since been decommissioned and is preserved as a family heirloom.
155. This site is located about 10 kilometres South of Somain.
156. This site is located about 5 kilometres Northwest of Somain.
157. This site is located 8 kilometres Northwest of Denain, and 1 kilometer West of Hélesmes.

158. Third Canadian Division, Seventh Infantry Brigade, Royal Canadian Regiment.
159. Amy Johnson would later become a very famous Aviator.
160. This site is located 4 kilometers to the Northwest.
161. LCol D.J. Goodspeed, *The Armed Forces of Canada 1867-1967*, Directorate of History, Canadian Forces Headquarters, Ottawa, 1967, p. 67.
162. CF. te Water, *Confederacy of the Nobles*; D11, p. 386-387.
163. Florence C. Estabrooks, *Estabrooks Family Vol 1*, p. 10.
164. Hugh Quinton's Diary, NB Museum Archives.
165. Raymond, "*The River St. John*", p. 280
166. Ven. Archdeacon Raymond, "*Pioneer Days at Saint John*," published in the Telegraph, April 1919.
167. Major Harold A. Skaarup is a Canadian Army Intelligence Branch officer stationed at the North American Aerospace Command (NORAD) facility on Cheyenne Mountain in Colorado Springs, Colorado since 1999. He is one of Walter and Elijah's many descendants who have served in the military.
168. From the Journal of Elijah Estabrooks, who was a Sergeant in Captain Israel Herrick's Company of Colonel Jedediah Prebble's Regiment of Provincials (Boston) during the 1758 campaign on Lake Champlain. He left Boston and later came to live on the St John River in 1763. He moved to Gagetown about 1775. (This was before the Loyalist invaders came and renamed the province after German George the Third's Brunswick, and then to make things worse put their boat on the NB flag.) Elijah died near Swan Creek, NB in August 1796.